Skeptic? Simple Answers Using Quran and Science

Dr. Eeshat Ansari

Skeptic? Simple Answers Using Quran and Science
Second Edition
Copyright © Eeshat Ansari 2023, 2022, 2021
eeshat11@yahoo.com
Cover artwork by Rudi Darmansyah
No part of this publication may be reproduced in any form, stored in a retrieval system, or transmitted in any form or by any means, without the prior written permission of the copyright owner, except as permitted by U.S. copyright law.

ISBN: (e-book)   978-1-7357409-5-9
ISBN: (Paperback) 978-1-7357409-6-6
ISBN: (Hardcover) 978-1-7357409-7-3

Dedicated to

My Mother and Father
Whom I remember as
Ammi and Abba

*They taught me how to love,
how to think and find the truth,
and how to have the courage to say what is true.*

**My Lord! Have mercy on them [parents] as they cared for me when
I was little** (17:24).

Table of Contents

THE SECRET OF SOLVING THE PARADOXES 1

THE SELF-REVELATIONS OF ALLAH 8

FREE WILL AND THE PREDESTINATION PARADOX 31

WHY DOES GOD ALLOW SUFFERING? (PART 1) 54

THE WATCHMAKER ANALOGY 63

THE OMNIPOTENCE QUESTION 71

THE THEORY OF EVOLUTION 80

APPENDIX - A 101

ACKNOWLEDGMENTS 113

NOTES 114

ONE

THE SECRET OF SOLVING THE PARADOXES

This Book Solves the Following Paradoxes:

1. If every action is predestined, how can humans have free will?

2. If every entity has a creator, who created God?

3. Why does a merciful God allow suffering?

4. Can God create an immovable stone He cannot move?

5. Is the theory of evolution compatible with the story of Adam and Eve?

SKEPTIC? SIMPLE ANSWERS USING QURAN AND SCIENCE

GOOD NEWS: THIS IS AN *EASY-TO-UNDERSTAND* BOOK

This book resolves centuries-old philosophical paradoxes *without drawing on Islamic philosophy or other philosophical traditions*. Instead, the book uses logic and verses from the Quran! Yes, the Quran already has answers backed by compelling arguments. Even atheist scholars would find it difficult to refute. Readers of all levels will find the book's straightforward and simple language easy to understand. For example, according to Muslim philosophers and scholars, the term *Al-Qadr* means "Allah knows everything and has already decided everything that will happen."[1] Instead of using the term *Al-Qadr*, this book uses the contemporary understandable word: 'predestination.' That is not all. This book goes on to explain, in plain English, what the term *predestination* stands for.

The new concepts presented here should appeal to readers of all faiths.

WHAT IS THE SECRET OF FINDING THE SOLUTIONS?

A close study of the Quran reveals that the 'human way of thinking' and 'logic used in the Quran' differ in many key areas. *This book uses the Quran's logic to solve paradoxes*. This strategy makes a big difference. Paradoxes can be explained in easy-to-understand language that appeals to human reasoning. If you reject evolution theory only because it clashes with religion while you disregard scientific facts, 21st-century audiences may remain skeptical. Many people interpret that science, in general, conflicts with Islam. This doubt interferes with Islamic belief. How can the Quran, which is the *word of Allah*, contradict science, which is *knowledge given by Allah*[2]?

QURAN: THE HOLY BOOK OF ISLAM

Muslims believe that the Quran is *the literal word of Allah*. It was revealed to Prophet Muhammad[PBUH] through the angel Gabriel over a period of approximately 23 years. No words were added or edited by the scribes. It is the ultimate source of guidance for Muslims. It includes topics such as Islamic belief, ethics, history, and eschatology. According to Muslims, the Quran does not contain contradictions and hasn't changed over time. The Quran is a miracle of Allah.

THE SECRET OF FINDING THE ANSWERS

> Bold letters are used in this book to indicate the English translation of Quranic verses. For example, please take a look at the English translation of verse 40:78 below.

THE QURAN USES DIFFERENT LOGIC

The following Quranic examples illustrate that humans have a different way of thinking than the Quran.

Islam is not a new religion. The very first human, Adam, was a Prophet of Islam. The Quran says: **"O Prophet [Muhammad**[PBUH]**], We [Allah] have sent many messengers before you"** (40:78).

> **USAGE OF THE PRONOUN 'WE' IN THE QURAN**
> In the above verse, Allah uses the pronoun 'We' instead of 'I' for Himself. Several languages, like Arabic, Urdu, Hindi, and English, sometimes use the majestic plural when the plural pronoun refers to a single person of authority. Such usage in English is called the 'royal we.'[3] For example: "We, the king of England..."

Prophet Muhammad[PBUH] (the superscript PBUH stands for *peace be upon him*) was the last Prophet, with many Prophets of Islam preceding him. According to verses (21:7-8), *every Prophet was human*. These Prophets were sent to different geographical regions during different periods.

Allah also gave holy books to some Prophets. **"He [Allah] sent down the Taurat (Torah) and the Injeel (Gospel)"** (3:3). Many Prophets described in the Quran are also mentioned in the Torah and Gospel. Muslims believe that parts of the old books (before the Quran) have been corrupted or lost. All Prophets were Muslims, and they preached only the religion of Islam. However, their books—and even the name of their religion—changed over time.

Here's a surprise: This is Not How Humans Think

There is a big difference between how the Quran is written and how humans write. For example, in the era of Prophet Muhammad[PBUH], tribal loyalties were essential to social cultures and political frameworks. It was a common tradition for desert dwellers to praise their families and tribes. Does the Quran also overtly praise Prophet Muhammad's[PBUH] tribe and family?

In the Quran, Allah mentions the names of and praises some Prophets. For example, the Quran mentions the *names* of and *praises* Prophet Abraham, his son Prophet Isaac, his grandson Prophet Jacob, and his great-grandson Prophet Joseph, peace be upon them (PBUT). The Quran also mentions the name of and praises Prophet Muhammad[PBUH]. But surprisingly, the names of Prophet Muhammad's[PBUH] grandfather, father, children, and grandchildren are *not in the Quran*. This includes grandchildren born during Prophet Muhammad's[PBUH] lifetime, while the Quran was being revealed to him. Nor are the names of the four-guided caliphs mentioned in the Quran, even though the four caliphs unconditionally supported the Prophet under extreme duress.

Similarly, the Quran mentions the name and praises Mary (mother of Prophet Jesus[PBUH]). There is even a chapter in the Quran titled 'Mary.' However, the Quran does not mention the names of Prophet Muhammad's[PBUH] grandmothers, mother, wives, daughters, and granddaughter. In pre-Islamic days of unconditional tribal loyalties, such omissions would have been beyond comprehension. Why were these names omitted? Only Allah knows the reason because the Quran says: **"Allah knows and *you [humans] do not know*"** (16:74). In other words, Allah made some part of knowledge beyond the ability of the human intellect to comprehend.

The Quran has an unusual way of assigning priorities. When we read the entire Quran, we realize that the Quran focuses on Allah's *message* given to different Prophets rather than *personal* details about the Prophets. Again, this is not the way humans think or write.

BACKGROUND OF PHILOSOPHICAL PARADOXES

Philosophical questions about the human relationship to the Divine originated long before Prophet Muhammad[PBUH]. For example, the Greek philosopher Epicurus (died 270 BCE) discussed the 'problem of evil.'[4] Similarly, 'Free will and predestination' is not a recent paradox. Back in the 7th or 8th centuries BCE, Homer's Odyssey addressed the same issue.[5] Still, to this day, such problems refuse to go away. Similarly, the rapid advance of science created new questions for the Abrahamic religions. For example, is the 'theory of evolution' compatible with the story of Adam and Eve?

Epicurus

Homer

SKEPTIC? SIMPLE ANSWERS USING QURAN AND SCIENCE

From laymen to scholars, no one can ignore the above philosophical paradoxes. In the absence of logical answers to these questions, many people become agnostic or atheist.

IDEOLOGICAL CONFLICTS

While responding to philosophical paradoxes, we noticed an ideological difference between the philosophical interpretation of God and the Islamic concept of God. Philosophers are free thinkers who proudly trample on conventional religious thinking. They may also severely criticize God.

However, the God-of-Islam cannot be discussed in the same manner. Unlike the God-of-philosophy, Muslims are supposed to always praise Allah in the best possible words like: "**All praise belongs to Allah, Lord of the worlds**" (1:2).

The second problem is that philosophers have total freedom to make extrapolations and guesses about the nature and attributes of the God-of-philosophy. Muslims, however, can only quote Allah's self-revelations as found in authentic Divine Islamic texts. The Quran prohibits Muslims from making wild guesses about Allah. Despite these conflicts, we can easily resolve the above paradoxes, including their most difficult objections. Furthermore, you'll soon discover that our solutions provide a complete and accurate picture instead of a distorted philosophical interpretation.

For example, philosophers may criticize the God-of-philosophy in the light of human suffering. But this approach only presents a partial picture of human life. The reality is that life consists of both challenging and happy times. The Quran says: "**Certainly, after every difficulty, there comes relief**" (94:6). Islam also teaches us how to face and overcome the emotional difficulties of our daily life. This reduces emotional suffering like stress, anger, fear, hopelessness, and depression. As a result, in a short time, a believer can return to a *peaceful state of mind*. People with such emotional stability are better equipped to face worldly challenges. In this book, while discussing evil and suffering, we will also discuss Islamic methods of overcoming negative emotions.

Later in this book, we will see several quotes from different philosophers. Those quotes by philosophers should not be used to interpret the God-of-Islam or Allah. *Subhan Allah* [Glory be to Allah]. He is above and beyond human criticism.

In this book, the terms 'Allah' and 'God-of-Islam' are used interchangeably due to sensitivity concerns. There is no difference in meaning between the two terms.

TWO

THE SELF-REVELATIONS OF ALLAH

WHY STUDY "ISLAMIC MONOTHEISM" TO SOLVE THE PARADOXES?

The five paradoxes discussed in the previous chapter have one common characteristic - they all try to understand or explain God. In this context, God can belong to any religion or ideology. However, this book offers a solution to the paradoxes based on Islamic ideology.

> We will solve the paradoxes using *Quranic logic*. However, to understand the Quranic logic, studying Islamic monotheism is essential.

STUDY OF THE "QURANIC LOGIC"

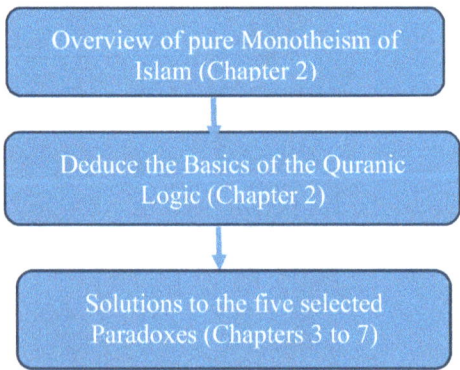

THE SELF-REVELATIONS OF ALLAH

IS THAT WHAT GOD LOOKS LIKE?

To worship God/gods, a believer must know how to perceive or imagine the unseen divine. For centuries humans have been asking, "What does the God/god look like?" This question is relevant to both monotheistic and polytheistic religions. About half a millennium *before* Christ, a Greek philosopher and poet, Xenophanes of Colophon (death 478 BCE), answered this question with pinpoint accuracy.

> Mortals deem that gods are begotten as they are,
> and have clothes like theirs and voice and form...
> yes, and if oxen and horses or lions had hands,
> and could paint with their hands,
> and produce works of art as men do,
> horses would paint the forms of gods like horses,
> and oxen like oxen
> the Ethiopians make their gods black and snub-nosed:
> the Thracians say theirs have blue eyes and red hair[6]

Xenophanes of Colophon

Xenophanes made perfect sense. The horse will think like a horse. For example, where are the better pastures, and who are the horse predators? A lion has no choice but to think like a lion. Of course, a human is bound to see the mythological world only from a human point of view. We cannot escape such dependency because it is an unshakeable and necessary part of our existence.

Even when we think outside the box, we are still constrained by the limitations of our human mind. For example, the human mind cannot comfortably imagine the infinite size of space surrounding the universe or time that continues forever. Similarly, the human mind cannot imagine any object that is *not similar to any other known or imaginable entity*. Based on this understanding, it is easy to predict what will happen when the human imagination creates or alters religion. In addition to looking like humans, all gods will also have male and female genders. Just like humans, gods and goddesses will give birth to offspring. Following human patterns, gods will also wear clothes and use verbal language to communicate.

The race and ethnicity of worshippers are also carried over to their gods. No wonder the African god Amun was dark-skinned, while the Norse goddess Iounn of Scandinavian mythology had blond hair.

Such transformation from a god to a human is called *anthropomorphism*. The Cambridge Dictionary defines anthropomorphism as "the showing or treating of animals, gods, and objects as if they are human in appearance, character, or behavior."[7] This book will use the word anthropomorphism only in the context of the *humanization of god/God*. Anthropomorphism helps believers visualize what they worship.

THE SELF-REVELATIONS OF ALLAH

Mayan mythical god, Kinich Ahau

Isis, goddess of life and magic

Here is a modern version of Xenophanes' prediction: according to spiritual author Eckhart Tolle[8]:

> "Man made 'God' in his own image. The eternal, the infinite, the unnamable was reduced to a mental idol that you had to believe in and worship as 'my god' or 'our god.'"

Many religions claim to be monotheistic, but the Islamic concept of God is unique. For example, Islam does not have the concept of 'son or daughter of God.' The Quran says: **He [Allah] begets not, nor is He begotten** (112:3).

UNIQUENESS OF ISLAMIC MONOTHEISM

To illustrate the exclusivity and uniqueness of Islamic monotheism, let us study the following excerpts from the Jewish Publication Societies' English Translation of the Jewish Bible, the Tanakh, 1917, the chapter of Genesis.[9]

32:25 And Jacob was left alone; and there wrestled a man with him until the breaking of the day.

32:26 And when he saw that he prevailed not against him, he touched the hollow of his thigh; and the hollow of Jacob's thigh was strained, as he wrestled with him.

32:27 And he said: 'Let me go, for the day breaketh.' And he said: 'I will not let thee go, except thou bless me.'

32:28 And he said unto him: 'What is thy name?' And he said: 'Jacob.'

32:29 And he said: 'Thy name shall be called no more Jacob, but Israel; for thou hast striven with God and with men and hast prevailed.'

32:30 And Jacob asked him and said: 'Tell me, I pray thee, thy name.' And he said: 'Wherefore is it that thou dost ask after my name?' And he blessed him there.

32:31 And Jacob called the name of the place Peniel: 'for I have seen God face to face and my life is preserved.'

According to these excerpts, God changed into human form and wrestled with Prophet Jacob[PBUH]. However, this interpretation is controversial. Encyclopedia Britannica states, "Jacob wrestled with a mysterious stranger, a *divine being* who changed Jacob's name to Israel."[10] Another interpretation says, "Jacob ultimately succeeded in pinning the *angel*, refusing to free him until he gives him a blessing."[11]

ISLAMIC MONOTHEISM

There is no surprise that so many religions follow Xenophanes' prediction. The reason is that humans are irresistibly attracted to imagine God as human or at least possessing human traits.

However, in Islam, God only has one role: role of God.

Suppose in some religion, God becomes a human, *even once*, the man-god will play a dual role:
(1) God as Lord and Sovereign.
(2) The role of a man who is perpetually and totally dependent on God for his survival.
Such duality violates the purity of Islamic monotheism.

Islam assigns the *highest priority* to monotheism and the uniqueness of Allah. To come into the fold of Islam, a person must recite the following declaration of faith with full sincerity and understanding:

> *La ilaha illAllah*
> *Muhammadur Rasulullah*

> Figuratively, this means:
> *there exists no god other than Allah.*
> Muhammad[PBUH] *is His messenger.*

The declaration of the Muslim faith highlights monotheism as its primary focus, making it *the most important message of Islam.*

The Quran emphasizes monotheism in different ways. Here are some examples:

Prophet Noah[PBUH] said: **"Worship *none* except Allah"** (11:26).

Prophet Joseph[PBUH] said: **"It is not fitting that we *attribute any partners* with Allah (and become polytheists)"** (12:38).

> Allah directly commands: **"No one else is *worthy of worship* except Me [Allah]"** (16:2).
>
> *The following sections demonstrate how the purity of Islamic monotheism is persistently preserved.*

NO ANTHROPOMORPHISM IN ISLAM

ISLAM STANDS OUT 1: GOD NEVER CONVERTS TO A HUMAN BEING

The Quran mentions the names of only 25 Prophets. Prophet Jacob[PBUH] is among those few individuals who are not only named but also praised in the Quran. **"Commemorate Our [Allah's] servants Abraham, Isaac, and *Jacob* (PBUT), possessors of Power and Vision"** (38:45). The Quran has stories about some Prophets similar to stories described in the Bible and Torah.

> Interestingly, the above-mentioned wrestling between Prophet Jacob[PBUH] and God (or an angel or other divine being) is *not* found in the Quran.

Allah never takes the shape of a human anywhere in the Quran—not even symbolically, figuratively, or metaphorically. Islam is free of anthropomorphism. Islam has one and exactly one divine being, and that is Allah. He is the creator of man. Here we see the striking contrast between the Quran and previous books.

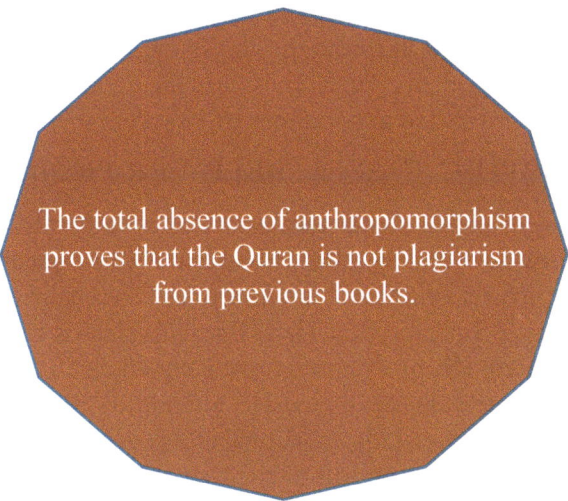

The total absence of anthropomorphism proves that the Quran is not plagiarism from previous books.

HUMAN CONTROL OVER DESTINY

Since prehistoric times, humans have longed to become the masters of their destiny by taking power away from the ever-unpredictable, all-powerful, unseen, and at times frightening and unknowable divine. One option is, as Xenophanes suggested, to believe in a god that takes human form. Such belief immediately removes the unseen and unknown aspects and places god entirely within the confines of human imagination. It allows idols and pictures of gods to be used in worship. Worshippers then have no problem imagining what the gods and goddesses look like.

THE CLASSIFICATIONS OF ANTHROPOMORPHISM

Throughout history, the strong desire to visualize the divine in the form of a human-god has profoundly influenced believers. There are three distinct ways humans have envisioned sharing divinity with gods:

ANTHROPOMORPHIC CASE 1: SCRIPTURED-GOD

In this type of human-god overlap, religious scripture or mythology states that a god took the shape of a created being. For example, a god or goddess may appear as a human or a combination of an animal and a human. Such transformation serves as a powerful attraction because the infinite and invisible power of the Creator becomes accessible through imagination and dreams. It seems easier to relate to and worship a human-god. This overlap is also called anthropomorphism, incarnation, personification, or manifestation of a god. Egyptian mythology has many gods and goddesses who look like human. This is the only case in which the initiative of human-god overlap comes from religious scripture or mythology and is *not* initiated in any manner by believers themselves.

ANTHROPOMORPHIC CASE 2: BELIEVER-PROJECTED-GOD

Sometimes the desire to worship a human-god motivates believers. In that case, devotees project onto their favorite priest the status of a god *without the priest's consent*. Imagine that High Priest Asklepios of the city temple is uniquely gifted. His profound religious knowledge and moving sermons attract thousands of devotees. He attends to the individual problems of his devotees by making emotional and passionate prayers to the idol of the temple god, which brings the devotees to tears. Instead of relating to the lifeless statue of the temple god, it is far more fulfilling to engage in two-way communication with Asklepios, who can answer questions, cry, offer an embrace, and provide moral support. As a result, interacting with an inspirational priest can be more rewarding than praying to idols.

How can the temple god ignore the intercession of a perfect worshipper like Asklepios? When Asklepios prayed for someone, and the prayers were answered, the believer would credit Asklepios, who acted as an intercessor, to plead the case to the temple god. Many worshippers started to believe that the temple god's help was not possible without the intervention of High Priest Asklepios. This is similar to the situation in which the fictional Aladdin possesses a magic lamp and is on your side. As a result, you can control the otherwise uncontrollable genie.

In this case, Asklepios never claimed to be the controller of the temple god. Instead, *the believers were responsible*. Instead of praying directly to a lifeless statue, the believers preferred to pray through a compassionate human intercessor to ensure that the temple god accepted their prayers.

After Asklepios' death, he became an even more effective intercessor of the temple god. Asklepios became an icon with legendary success stories. Believers began to pray to the soul of Asklepios to act as an intercessor to the temple god.

Unlike a petition from an ordinary believer, the temple god cannot refuse Asklepios. In other words, Asklepios was granted the status of *controlling-intercessor* to the temple god. As far as inner perception is concerned,

Asklepios is a deity, and while seeking Asklepios' help, even mentioning the name of the temple god is no longer necessary.

The only way to raise Asklepios' status from man to god is to encourage his followers to praise and love Asklepios *repeatedly*. Here it should be noted that the praise-and-love cycle plays a critical role. Loving the holy man develops a sense of closeness and trust in him while showering him with exaggerated praise makes him appear superior to ordinary humans.

After several sessions of praise-and-love cycles, the followers raise the status of the holy man far above ordinary humans, and gradually the idea of his divinity becomes part of their belief. The entire process bears a striking resemblance to the custom of 'ancestor veneration' practiced in many cultures.

ANTHROPOMORPHIC CASE 3: SELF-PROCLAIMED-GOD

Sometimes, instead of the believers, Asklepios can exploit an opportunity by claiming to be the controlling-intercessor, and the temple god cannot refuse his prayers. In other words, Asklepios self-proclaims divine status. He can even start a cult of his own. For centuries, Egyptian pharaohs claimed to be gods.

ISLAM STANDS OUT 2: PREVENTING BELIEVER-PROJECTED-GOD AND SELF-PROCLAIMED-GOD

Ever since the Prophets introduced Islam to humanity, there was a risk that future generations of Muslims may be inclined to ascribe divine attributes to their chosen Prophet, saint, or sacred character. The Quran emphatically prohibits this in multiple ways.

> "Surely our Lord's Majesty is exalted: He has neither taken a *wife nor a son*" (72:3)

The above verse 72:3 rules out any possibility of the believer-projected-god scenario, where followers promote a Prophet or holy man as an offspring of God or make a holy woman God's spouse.

The Quran not only describes Prophets as human but also points out their human limitations, thus guiding the believers to stay in touch with reality and avoid the believer-projected-god scenario. The only difference between the Prophets and other humans was that the Prophets received divine inspiration to guide them toward Islam: **"the Prophets that We [Allah] had sent before you [O Muhammad^{PBUH}] were only men to whom We had given revelation…We did not give them bodies that could survive without food, nor were they immortal"** (21:7–8). Please note that the verse places all Prophets on the same level as the rest of mortal humans, including their dependency on food to survive.

All humans are slaves (or servants) of Allah. *Here, the meaning of the word slave has changed.* This meaning has nothing to do with human trafficking or forced labor. Instead, in verses 21:7–8, the word *slave* means that all humans can act only by the will of Allah because He maintains continuous total control of the entire universe in every aspect. In other words, all humanity has a 100 percent helpless puppet-like dependence on Allah for every physical movement. In that sense, all of us continuously follow the commands of Allah [The role of free will is discussed later]. We cannot act independently on our own. Therefore, all humanity is a slave of Allah.

The Quran describes several incidents when Allah guided the Prophets, answered their questions, and encouraged them during calamities. Humans have limited knowledge; therefore, sometimes, we make wrong choices. The Quran relates some incidents in which the Prophets, too, made mistakes in judgment, and after they repented, Allah forgave them. Muslims believe that on 'the Day of Judgment', all humans will be raised from the dead then Allah will judge how people will spend their afterlife. On that day, Allah will judge every Prophet, along with the rest of humanity.

> In Islam, the roles of God (as Lord and Sovereign) and humans (as His helplessly dependent slaves) are *never* reversed or overlapped.

Although the Prophets were human, their significance was not reduced as they brought Allah's guidance to the people. Allah sent the Prophet^{PBUH} with two essential purposes—to give humanity the Quran and the Hadith. The term *Hadith* (plural: *ahadith*) is defined as: "the traditions relating to the deeds and utterances of the Prophet as recounted by the companions [Muslims who saw Prophet Muhammad^{PBUH} during his life]."[12] This included the tacit endorsements or disapproval made by the Prophet

Muhammad^PBUH. The Quran says to Prophet Muhammad^PBUH: **"Allah has revealed to you the *Book* and *wisdom*, and taught you what you did not know"** (4:113). So Prophet Muhammad^PBUH not only conveyed to us the Quran but also explained its meaning and other details in the form of ahadith.

It is interesting to note that no single Prophet monopolized the attention of the Quran. That would have encouraged believers to promote the overtly praised or discussed Prophet as believer-projected-god. Instead, the Quran conveys stories of several Prophets. For example, as many as 98 verses in chapter 12 of the Quran relate the story of Prophet Joseph^PBUH. The Quran also contains chapters named after the Prophets Joseph, Noah, Jonah, Hud, Abraham, and Muhammad (PBUT).

All Prophets had exactly the same mission—to teach Islam: **"to every Prophet whom We sent before you [O Muhammad^PBUH], We [Allah] revealed the same Message: *'there is no god but Me [Allah], so worship Me Alone.'"*** (21:25). This includes Prophet Jesus^PBUH, who preached Islam and said: **"I am indeed a *slave* of Allah"** (19:30). His followers were also Muslims. **"When Jesus^PBUH found out that people had no faith, he asked: 'Who will help me in the cause of Allah?' The disciples replied: 'We will help you in the cause of Allah. We believe in Allah. Be our witness that *we are Muslims*' [we submit to Allah]"** (3:52).

In the Quran, Allah praises some Prophets. Again, all praise is not directed toward just one Prophet. And the praise is never exaggerated; it does not project any Prophet into the human-god-overlap zone. For example: **"The *slave of Allah* Prophet Job ... was full of patience. He was an excellent devotee"** (38:41–44). In verse (33:56), Allah praised Prophet Muhammad^PBUH.

The Quran says: **"among the Prophets, We [Allah] have exalted some above others"** (2:253). Instead of paying full attention only to the personalities of the Prophets, Muslims should focus on the Prophets' messages. **"Say (Oh Muslims): 'We believe in Allah and that which is revealed to us; and what was revealed to Abraham, Ishmael, Isaac, Jacob, and their descendants and that which was given to Moses, Jesus, and other Prophets from their Rabb (Allah). *We do not make a distinction between them*"** (2:136) (PBUT).

The Quran's strong emphasis that all Prophets were men should be sufficient to prevent any human from trying to become a self-proclaimed-god.

NO INDIRECT ANTHROPOMORPHISM IN ISLAM

ISLAM STANDS OUT 3: ALL PRAYERS ARE MADE **ONLY** TO ALLAH

> The Quran contains dozens of prayers; each prayer is addressed exclusively to Allah and no one else.

For example, Prophet Moses[PBUH] called for help *directly* from Allah. **"O Lord! Surely I am in desperate need of whatever good You may send down to me"** (28:24).

No prayer in the Quran is made to an intercessor. In the above prayer, Prophet Moses[PBUH] did not ask his predecessor Prophet Abraham[PBUH] for help, nor his soul, to pray to Allah on his behalf. Unlike the Tanakh verses discussed above, not a single prayer in the Quran is made to an angel, mysterious stranger, or divine being other than Allah.

While a believer is *alive*, he or she can pray for others: **"O Allah! Guide us to the right way"** (1:6). This verse is a prayer for 'us' which means all humanity. Islam also allows believers to request a living person to pray for a justified cause. Regarding worldly tasks (like passing salt or opening a door), Muslims are allowed to seek help from any suitable person. Here, the helping person must be alive, listening, and capable of helping. Why? So that the helper is perceived only as human and not as a divine being. Of course, people can and should also seek Allah's help in worldly affairs. Nonetheless, they should still exert maximum effort to achieve their earthly objectives.

ISLAM STANDS OUT 4: ONLY ALLAH HAS THE AUTHORITY TO REWARD WITH HEAVEN OR PUNISH WITH HELL

One question remains unanswered. All over the world, why are so many people converting to Islam, even if Islam does not rely on the popularity of idol worship and anthropomorphism?

The following incident gives a hint. During the early years of his prophethood, Prophet Muhammad[PBUH] and a few hundred Muslims migrated to the city of Medina. However, Muslims were constantly threatened and attacked by pagans from Mecca, who greatly outnumbered Muslims. One of the major pagan attacks resulted in the Battle of Uhud. In this battle, Muslims suffered heavy casualties, and Prophet Muhammad[PBUH] was seriously injured. His face was covered in blood. At this challenging moment, Prophet Muhammad[PBUH] commented that the pagans injured their Prophet, who preached to them about monotheism. *How can such people succeed on the Day of Judgment?*[13] Immediately, the following verse from the Quran was revealed to the Prophet[PBUH]: **"O Prophet, it is not for you to decide; it is up to Allah whether He pardons or punishes them since they are wrongdoers"** (3:128).

You do not have to be a psychologist to realize that any human at such a desperate moment would readily be consumed by self-pity, anger, fear, and revenge. In such a situation, no human can think of a verse like the one above. Only Allah, who controls reward and punishment, could reveal such words.

In Islam, Allah and only Allah, and no one else but Allah, is the ultimate judge who can punish or reward. No human can reward heaven or accept anyone's prayers. As much as humans may desire to do so, they cannot take over this authority from Allah. Allah may forgive a person and inform a Prophet to convey information to believers. But no pious man, not even a Prophet, can independently forgive sins. On the Day of Judgment, Allah will judge every human, *including the Prophets*. People are converting to Islam because it is God's true religion, not a man-made religion. No wonder Islam is free from anthropomorphism.

ISLAM STANDS OUT 5: NO HUMAN CAN OVERPOWER ALLAH OR HIS ANGELS

At times, a person may outsmart or fool others. In some Xenophanic religions (based on Xenophanes' model discussed above), this human behavior is also present among gods. For example, in Greek mythology, an ordinary woman, Arachne, challenged Athena, the goddess of wisdom and crafts, to a weaving contest and defeated the goddess.

Allah is not like a human in any way. There is no incident in the Quran in which a human outsmarts, overpowers, or competes with God-of-Islam. The Quran says, **"you [humans] cannot challenge God in the heavens or the earth"** (29:22). Allah is the Creator and Controller of all humans and angels.

Muslims do not worship angels or consider them to be divine beings. Allah is the creator of the angels. Similar to Prophet Jacob's[PBUH] incident mentioned above, the Quran does not describe any incident in which a human overpowers an angel because that would be dominating the command of Allah.

ISLAM STANDS OUT 6: ISLAM DOES NOT PERMIT THE WORSHIP OF HEAVENLY BODIES OR *ANY* ENTITY FROM HUMAN IMAGINATION

When humans imagine or alter a religion, they may add an impressive or frightening entity as a deity. For example, the Egyptian Pharaoh Akhenaten (1364–1347 BCE) worshipped the sun god. Many ancient religions worshipped stars, the moon, or the sun because they appeared eternal and impressive. However, Islam explicitly *prohibits* their worship. **"Do not prostrate yourself before the Sun or the moon;** *rather prostrate yourself before Allah"* (41:37).

That is not all; the Quran strictly prohibits adding anything out of human imagination as a deity (e.g., a combination of human and animal):

> There is *nothing* similar to Him [Allah] (42:11)

Whenever humans imagine an entity, they are likely to draw inspiration from something they already know or can imagine. Since Allah is unlike anything humans are familiar with, humans are unable to even *imagine* what Allah is like.

That is why mosques have no statue, image, or picture of God-of-Islam. Even statues, pictures, or paintings of Prophets are not allowed because that could encourage a believer-projected-god scenario. For example, here is the picture of the interior of the Great Mosque in Sousse:

Great Mosque in Sousse, Tunisia

THE UNIQUE CONCEPT OF GOD IN ISLAM

HOW TO LEARN ABOUT ALLAH?

Allah is beyond human imagination. *Therefore, we cannot learn about Allah through guesswork.* The Quran tells us that every piece of knowledge, worldly or spiritual, is also controlled by Allah. **"They [humans] cannot access anything out of His [Allah's] knowledge except what He pleases"** (2:255). The verse states that He allows humans only limited access to knowledge. In other words, Allah has complete and constant control over knowledge and humans' ability to access it. Acquiring knowledge about Allah is possible only through His self-revelations.

WHO CREATED THE GOD OF ISLAM?

In the early years of Islam, some pagans asked Prophet Muhammad[PBUH], "What is the ancestry of your God?"[14] This question is a typical example of trying to explain God in human terms. At that time, the following four Quran verses were revealed to Prophet Muhammad[PBUH]. These verses constitute chapter 112 of the Quran, called *Al Ikhlaas*.

> **Say: Allah is God the One**; [1]
> **God is the Self-Sufficient** [independent of all, while everything else depends on Him]; [2]
> **He begets not, nor is He begotten;** [3]
> **And there is none comparable to Him.** [4]

SKEPTIC? SIMPLE ANSWERS USING QURAN AND SCIENCE

Here is a verse-by-verse explanation:

Verse 1: English orientalist E. H. Palmer translated this verse as: **"Say: God is alone."** In verse (4:82), the Quran says it contains no contradiction anywhere! This means that if the Quran says that "God is one and only," then the Quran will never say, 'Such a saint is also God,' or, 'Include certain pious men into divinity, and God will still remain one.'

Verse 2: The previous verse used the Arabic word *ahad* to describe Allah. However, this word may be misunderstood as referring to loneliness, often seen as a human vulnerability. Verse 2 clears this doubt by telling us that Allah is self-sufficient *in every way*. In contrast to humans, Allah does not depend on air, water, food, or sleep. He does not possess the emotional weaknesses of exhaustion, boredom, depression, or loneliness. Allah is not only the Creator but also the Sustainer of the universe. All matter and energy are entirely dependent on Allah.

The following Hadith gives an idea of Allah's infinite capability and majesty. Allah says that if all humanity becomes as pious as the best human (say, like Prophet Muhammad[PBUH]), it will still not increase Allah's kingdom in any way. Similarly, if humanity becomes as wicked as the worst person (for example, the pharaoh), Allah's kingdom will not decrease in any way. If Allah fulfills *every* single wish of *all humanity*, the kingdom of Allah will not decrease even as much as a sea decrease when a needle is dipped and raised.[15] With this in mind, when the above verse says Allah is self-sufficient, *believe it*!

Interestingly, the example from the above Hadith does not say if a 'spoon' is dipped into the sea because a spoon has a concave cavity to hold water. Similarly, the example does not say a 'thread' is dipped into the sea because a thread can soak up some water. Instead, the example uses a needle, which neither has any cavity nor the capability to absorb water.

Verse 3: This verse explains that Allah has no offspring, nor is He the offspring of anyone. Reproduction is an essential characteristic of all life forms created by Allah. All animals have limited lifespans. Therefore, reproduction is the only way to perpetuate species. Except for species like bacteria, most animals require a father and a mother to produce a child. Parents influence many characteristics of their offspring, like race, height, weight, and DNA. Reproduction continues across generations as long as the species lasts. It must be noted that the father and mother are not the creators of the baby, but their bodies make the baby.

The Quran presents another argument: **"Praise be to Allah, the One Who has begotten no son and Who has no partner in His Kingdom; nor is He helpless to need a protector [unlike a human who needs a son/daughter as supporter and protector in old age]"** (17:111). In other words, why does the everlasting, all-knowing, omnipotent, fully-contented God need a son? Did God lack anything the son could provide? God does not get old or weak. Don't forget that reproduction is an animal-level dependency. How could the Supreme God be dependent, just like His creation? Further, if you accept that God has offspring, the offspring will share God's divinity. This means God can no longer be one and alone, as in verse 1.

The verse also says that Allah is not anyone's offspring. Allah created all lifeforms and gave them the ability to reproduce. But this characteristic does not apply to Allah. This should not come as a surprise because the above quoted verse 42:11 says there is nothing like Allah.

Verse 4: This verse unequivocally rules out the possibility that anyone or anything can be *similar* to Allah. He is without any competition, challenge, or partnership of any kind. No human can compete with Allah (unlike Arachne, who challenged the goddess Athena).

Since nothing resembles Allah, worshipping anything that claims similarity to Allah is prohibited. Therefore, a Muslim cannot imagine Allah in the symbolic form of a statue, idol, picture, Prophet, or holy man. This leaves the Muslim with only one option—to *worship Allah directly* and none other.

Verse 4 rules out the possibility of all *indirect* ways of acquiring knowledge about God through a God like being. For example, a student pilot can learn to fly a plane from a flight simulator but to worship Allah, a similar approach cannot work.

Muslim philosopher and theologian Abu Hamid al-Ghazali (death: 1111) said about Allah: "He is not a body with a form, or a limitary, quantitative substance, not resembling bodies in quantifiability or divisibility, or in being a substance or qualified by a substance.... He does not resemble anything that exists, nor anything that exists resembles Him. There is nothing whatsoever like unto Him, nor is He like unto anything. He is not delimited by magnitude, contained in places, encompassed by directions, or bounded by Heavens or Earth...."[16]

> The above four verses prove that Allah's attributes are unique and entirely *different from human characteristics.*

THE QURAN ENCOURAGES US TO PONDER ABOUT SOME SUBJECTS

The Quran encourages readers to ponder and explore Allah's creation and look for the signs (*ayaat*) that prove the infinite capability and power of the Creator. After all, a subset of Allah's creation is within reach of our observation and scientific exploration. The following verse is an example:

"**In the Earth, there are [different types of] tracts [of land] side by side: gardens of grapes, cornfields, and palm trees with single and double trunks -** *they are all watered with the same water,* **yet We make some of them excel others in taste. Surely in this,** *there are signs for people who reflect*" (13:4).

THE QURAN *PROHIBITS* US FROM THINKING ABOUT SOME SUBJECTS

Human imagination is limited. When a human makes a guess, it has to be similar to something s/he already knows or can imagine. But nothing is similar to Allah. Therefore, all our guesses about Allah are *guaranteed* to be wrong. To avoid guesswork, Muslims are supposed to learn about Allah only from His self-revelations, as found in the Quran and Hadith. In addition, the Quran strictly prohibits us from making *wild guesses* about Allah: **"Has Allah indeed permitted you or do you invent [ideas] to attribute to Allah?"** (10:59).

> It is strictly prohibited to make wild guesses or extrapolations about Allah.

ATTRIBUTES OF ALLAH – WITHOUT ANTHROPOMORPHISM

The Quran provides another way for believers to relate to Allah, who is absolute in the true sense. This method is also without a trace of anthropomorphism.

The Quran describes Allah by His *attributes*. All attributes are easily understandable, even by illiterates. For example, one of the attributes or names of Allah is *the* **All-Seeing** [42:11].

However, it is imperative that attributes of Allah must be interpreted in the light of the verse ***"there is nothing like Him"*** (42:11). Therefore, the attribute of *the All-Seeing* should never be interpreted in human terms or in terms of anything we can imagine. Otherwise, two Quran verses (*All-Seeing* and 'there is nothing like Him') would contradict. In addition, our interpretation of the All-Seeing should suit the majesty of the Creator of the universe and be in line with other attributes of Allah.

CAREFUL, IT'S ONLY A SIMILE

Sometimes, the Quran uses human-understandable similes. What if a reader misinterprets the simile in human terms? The verse ***"there is nothing like Him"*** (42:11) adequately warns against such anthropomorphism. The Quran also takes one additional step. The following verse *explicitly* informs the reader that (1) the Quran contains similes and (2) warns against their misinterpretation. It is a very informative verse. To properly explain its meaning, I have divided it into three segments: beginning, middle, and end.

> **He is the One Who has revealed to you the Book. Some of its verses are decisive [word *muhkamat* used here] - they are the *foundation* of the Book - while others are symbolic or allegorical [*mutashabihat*]** [beginning of the verse].
>
> **Those whose hearts are infected with disbelief follow the allegorical part to mislead others and to give it their own interpretation, seeking its hidden meanings. But no one knows its hidden meanings except Allah** [middle of the verse].
>
> **Those who are *well grounded in knowledge* say: "We believe in it; it is all from our Lord" None will take heed except the people of understanding"** (3:7)[17] [end of the verse].

SKEPTIC? SIMPLE ANSWERS USING QURAN AND SCIENCE

The beginning segment of 3:7 divides Quranic verses into two groups: **decisive** *(muhkamat)* and **symbolic/allegorical** *(mutashabihat)*. The decisive verses *(muhkamat)* clearly have one meaning. They constitute the foundation of Islam. For example, the four verses of the Quran's chapter Al Ikhlaas, discussed earlier in this chapter.

Some Quranic verses have symbolic meanings *(mutashabihat)*. For example, verses using the name of Allah *the All-Seeing*. Through such symbolism, we can gain a limited understanding of Allah.

The middle segment of the above verse warns that some people misguide others using symbolic verses. For example, misinterpreting the Allah's attribute, *the All-Seeing*, in human terms. When this happens, human limitations are imposed on the Supreme God. The middle segment prohibits guesswork about Allah by *speculating on hidden meanings*.

The final segment of this verse offers three essential concepts.

1. **A Muslim should understand the foundation of Islam**. Decisive verses are unambiguous. Words contained in such verses clearly convey their message leaving no room for guesswork. For example, "**Allah is One**" (112:1). Such verses are the foundation of Islam. The Quran credits people who know the difference between decisive and allegorical verses, calling them well-grounded in knowledge.

2. **The middle and final segments imply that a Muslim has the authority to reject any scholar's interpretation that conflicts with the foundation of Islam**. Once you know the foundation of Islam, then you are in a position to evaluate the claim made by any scholar as to what the Quran says between the lines or about its hidden meanings. The entire verse also implies that ordinary Muslims have the authority to detect and discard misinterpretations proposed by anyone, including scholars. This limits the control of Islamic religious scholars over society. The authority to judge and the responsibility of judgment are passed on to the individual Muslim. For example, if a scholar recommends worshipping another god besides Allah or along with Allah, the scholar's teaching can be rejected because it contradicts the monotheistic belief. The last segment of this verse encourages us to reflect and ponder so we can make the right decisions. Islam is not just a bunch of do's and don'ts. It is a lifelong spiritual journey of self-improvement, including introspection and pondering that leads to the right choices.

3. **While rejecting the human interpretation of hidden meanings, we should continue to believe what is written in the Quran as it is.** The Quran's symbolic verse should not be rejected. Instead, accept what the Quran says as it is. Muslims do not have to know the hidden meaning.

For example, accept the attribute the All-Seeing. Only reject interpretations that suggest that this attribute of Allah is similar to a human or any other creature. Muslim theologian Ibn Taymiyyah (death: 1328) advised how to interpret similes in the Quran: *"without misinterpreting [the text], without divesting [God of His attributes], without asking how and without comparing [God to His Creation]."*[18]

Ibn Taymiyyah

Since Allah is beyond human imagination, our languages do not contain words to describe Allah. Isn't it amazing how the Quran solves the impossible problem of the limitations of human vocabulary and comprehension by describing the unimaginable Allah using similes? At the same time, it is a test for us because we are responsible for rejecting scholars who try to convert Islam into a Xenophanic religion or make other mistakes.

HOW TO DISTINGUISH THE MUHKAMAT AND MUTASHABIHAT VERSES?

Let us evaluate the following three verses:

All the bounty is in the Hand of Allah (3:73)
Patient men, desirous [to look at] of the Face of their Lord, who perform the prayer … (13:22)
Construct the ship under Our [Allah's] Eyes (23:27).

If we interpret the above verses in anthropomorphic terms and assume they are decisive (muhkamat), our interpretation would contradict the verse **"There is nothing similar to Him [Allah]"** (42:11). Such an interpretation cannot be accepted because the Quran contains no contradictions. Therefore, the verses cannot be *muhkamat*.

So the only other option is to interpret that the above three verses are *mutashabihat*, and therefore the face, eyes, and hand are just similes. So how do Allah's face, eyes, and hand look? As suggested by the above verse (3:7), this question has only one answer, "we do not know," because the Quran says: **"Surely Allah knows and you [humans] do not know"** (16:74). Our knowledge is limited. For sure, His face, eyes, and hand are not like humans or any known object. We should believe, just like idioms, that the messages the verses convey are true. We do not have the full details.

> Mutashabihat verses (or similes) do not imply that Islam has anthropomorphism.

Is 'Human Logic' Applicable to Allah?

Allah is not similar to humans in any way. The Quran says: **"Subhan-Allah"** (16:1), or Allah, is pure and free from human limitations or anthropomorphic associations. Here, the term *human logic* means "the way humans think, conceptualize, analyze, and draw a conclusion." Human mental behavior or *human logic* cannot be projected onto the God-of-Islam. Unless specified in the Quran and Hadith, humans cannot predict how Allah makes decisions or what Allah can or cannot do. Therefore, we can conclude that *if a task is impossible for humans, it does not mean the same task is impossible for the God-of-Islam.*

> Human logic is not applicable to Allah.

THREE

FREE WILL AND THE PREDESTINATION PARADOX

PREDESTINATION

This belief is based on the concept of an Omniscient God who *knows* everything that has ever happened, is happening, and will ever happen in the future. Additionally, God is Omnipotent, which means He has total, continuous, and absolute control over *all events, movements, and actions*. God also compels and coerces *all* human activities. Therefore, God predetermines who will go to heaven and who will go to hell. This concept, however, leads to a difficult question: 'if only God can make events happen, humans cannot be held responsible for their actions. What is the justification of divine punishment?'

FREE WILL

In contrast, the 'free will' ideology assumes that instead of God, every human has the freedom to choose between good and evil actions (assuming there is no predestination). Thus, the individual becomes fully responsible for his/her actions. The role of God is only to determine whether a person's actions merit entry into heaven or condemnation to hell.

> However, this concept leads to another challenging question, 'if individuals have total freedom to choose their actions, how can God be Omnipotent?'
>
> *The above two definitions suggest that predestination and free will are mutually exclusive.*

In doubt

EXAMPLE OF FREE WILL AND PREDESTINATION PARADOX?

Ted Bundy was a serial killer. A Florida court found him guilty of murdering more than 30 women. He was executed in 1989. His case is referenced here only to elucidate the ever-controversial 'free will and predestination' paradox.

Bundy was born out of wedlock and had an unhappy childhood. His birth and upbringing were out of his control. Given his background, was Bundy predestined to commit these murders, or did he have a choice to avoid them? Many children are born out of wedlock, yet they do not grow up to become serial killers. Did genetic factors compel Bundy to commit murders (biological determinism)? If so, would he still face divine punishment?

Everyone faces similar, albeit generally less extreme, questions in our daily lives when we try to make sense of uncontrollable and alarming threats around us. Fear of an unpredictable future drives the popularity of astrology and superstition (like a broken mirror that causes bad luck). Which calamities are *meant to be,* and what can we change with our *efforts?* Throughout history, these questions have attracted both theist and atheist scholars and philosophers, as well as ordinary people. Theists have offered a broad spectrum of explanations, from stoic causal determinism to dialogues between Zeus and Odysseus. Elaborate rationalizations have been provided that God's knowledge of our future does not interfere with human free will.

Free Will and Predestination Paradox in Muslim History

Historically, Muslims have also struggled with the issue of 'free will and predestination.' According to BBC Bitesize, "All Muslims believe that God has given human beings free will, but different Muslims have different beliefs about the limits of free will."[19] In the 8th and 10th centuries, Mu'tazilites believed that "humans must have total free will as God…"[20] Therefore, humans are fully responsible for their choices. While Asharites rejected "the Mu'tazilites' views about free will."[21] The disagreement resulted in many violent confrontations, and the Muslim community, on the whole, paid a heavy price.

Einstein's Argument

In 1939, Albert Einstein wrote an article regarding the relationship between religion and science, in which he commented: "If this being is omnipotent, then every occurrence, including every human action, every human thought, and every human feeling and aspiration is also His work; how is it possible to think of holding a man responsible for their deeds and thoughts before such an almighty Being? In giving out punishments and rewards, He would, to a certain extent, be *passing judgment on Himself.* How can this be combined with the goodness and righteousness ascribed to Him?"[22]

> Einstein's comment puts theists of all religions in a challenging position. They are forced to defend the existence of free will; otherwise, they cannot justify the divine punishment.

Einstein's argument and Xenophanic Religions

Einstein's above argument makes perfect sense for all the Xenophanic religions. When a religion claims that a god became human, this statement inherently enforces human limitations and restrictions on the god. It means that, just like an ordinary human, the god also has skeletal, circulatory, nervous, muscular, respiratory, endocrine, immune, urinary, integumentary, reproductive, and digestive systems. Just like humans, god's DNA is also made from nucleotides. Otherwise, do not say *God is a man*.

> **HUMAN LOGICAL LIMITATIONS**
> Once you accept that a god is bound by human physical limitations, it makes sense to assume that God is also constrained by humans' logical limitations! Therefore, *if some task is impossible for humans to imagine, it is also impossible for God to imagine or do.* That is why, Einstein argued, "If this being is omnipotent, then every occurrence, including every human action, every human thought, and every human feeling and aspiration is also His work." Einstein concluded that if God is omnipotent then it is impossible to imagine that humans are responsible for their actions or have free will.
> Since Xenophanic god is also bound by human limitations (see above example of 12 anatomical systems), therefore, human-god cannot make predestination to coexist with free will. In conclusion, in all Xenophanic religions, free will cannot exist along with predestination. In Xenophanic religions, to prove otherwise, especially in the context of the predestination-free will paradox, requires a great deal of linguistic artistry.

WHAT DOES THE QURAN SAY ABOUT FREE WILL AND PREDESTINATION?

The Quran *simultaneously supports both* free will and predestination:

Support of predestination in the Quran: The following verses tell us that Allah fully controls human fate: "**God leads astray or guides to the right path whomever He wants**" (6:39) and "**whatever hardships you face on earth and in your souls were written in the Book before the creation of souls**" (57:22).

Support of free will in the Quran: The Quran also says that humans have free will to choose between good and evil: **"O Prophet, proclaim: 'The truth is from your Lord.' Then whosoever wills, let him believe, and whosoever wills, let him disbelieve"** (18:29) and "act as you wish" (41:40).

FREE WILL AND THE PREDESTINATION PARADOX

> ## IS THAT A CONTRADICTION?
> In this context, Brill's Encyclopedia concludes: "particular Quranic passages provided *fertile ground for arguments in support of and against human free will.*"[23]

Another verse says that the Quran does not have a contradiction: **"Will they not ponder on the Quran? Had it not come from someone other than God, they would have certainly found therein many contradictions"** (4:82).

How do we reconcile the above verses (6:39) and (18:29), which seem to contradict in the context of predestination and free will?

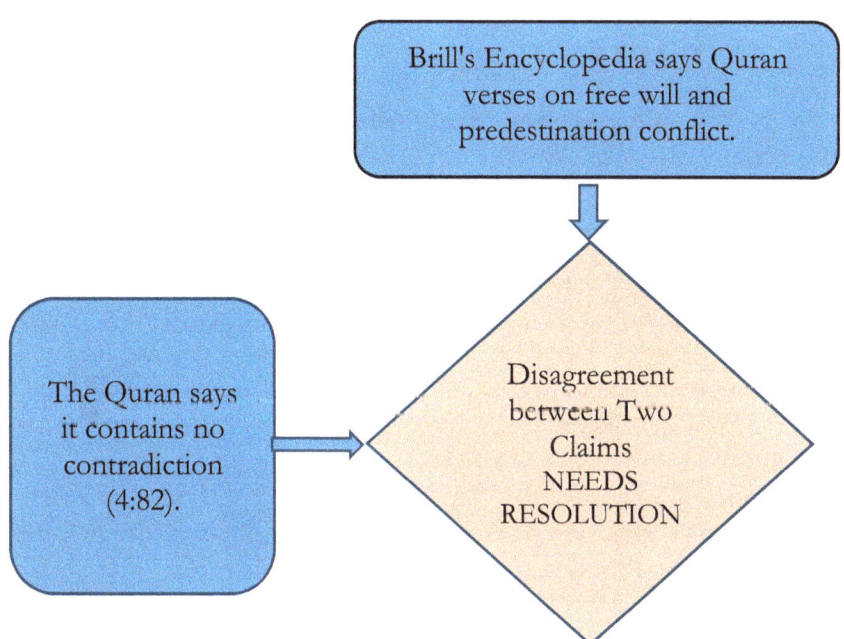

ISLAMIC POINT OF VIEW OF THE PARADOX
Islam makes the following distinction:

Difference between Intention and Action
Suppose you intend to make a fist with your right hand and successfully do it. This means Allah allowed you to fulfill your intention. An individual with a disabled right hand would not be able to act upon the same intention. In that case, Allah did not permit the action. Allah either makes the event occur or He prevents it. However, human intention is the *initial step*. Beyond that point, Allah decides if the event will or will not occur. So, *human intentions play a crucial role*.

However, Allah is *always* the Doer behind the scenes: "**Allah has created you and what you make**" (37:96). According to Muslim philosopher and thinker Abu-l-Hasan al-Ash`ari (death: 936 CE) "Actions of human beings are created (*makhluq*) by God, the creatures [including humans] are not capable of creating any action."[24] This leads to some interesting questions: do we become a sinner as soon as have an evil thought? Will we be rewarded for our good thoughts?

Good News: We Are Not Responsible for Our *Involuntary* Evil Thoughts

Let us be honest. We do not have control over our random thoughts. This leads to the question: "will we be punished for our involuntary evil thoughts"? The answer is no. Allah is fair and just. The Prophet[PBUH] said, "Allah has forgiven my nation for the evil suggestions of their hearts, so long as they *do not act upon it* or *speak of it*, and for *what they are forced to do*."[25] A person who intends to sin becomes a sinner as soon as they take the first step towards it or talk about it.

The Prophet[PBUH] said, "If two Muslims take out their swords to *fight each other*, then *both of them* will be from amongst the people of the hellfire." It was asked of the Prophet, 'It is alright for the killer, but what about the killed one?' He replied, "The killed one had the *intention* to kill his opponent."[26] Here, the Prophet[PBUH] is describing the judgment of Allah. It must be noted that humans do not think in this fashion.

What about good intentions? Allah is most generous. He may reward us for good intentions, even for non-religious acts, or, at times, without doing any action at all. The Prophet[PBUH] said, "If a man spends on his family sincerely for Allah's sake, then it is an alms-giving reward for him."[27] In summary:

FREE WILL AND THE PREDESTINATION PARADOX

> The Prophet^{PBUH} said, "The reward of deeds depends on the intention." (Sahih Al-Bukhari 1.51)

Acts of Worship Performed with Improper Intention

A human judge declares a suspect guilty based on his/her illegal actions. Allah has entirely different judgment criteria. Allah has complete knowledge of all our intentions and actions. So Allah's decision is primarily based on our intentions. The following Hadith explains the significance of intentions:

On the Day of Judgment, Allah would judge a man who would claim, "I fought for you [O Allah] until I died as a martyr." Allah would say, "You have told a lie. You fought so that people called you a brave warrior and were called so [in this world]." Similarly, another person would claim he acquired knowledge, taught others, and recited the Quran. Again, Allah would reject the claim because man's primary goal was not to please Allah but to get worldly recognition as a scholar, and Allah gave him recognition in the world itself.

A third person may claim that he generously donated wealth to charity. Again, Allah would judge that person as a liar because, instead of pleasing Allah, that man's primary goal was to gain worldly recognition as a generous donor, and he was recognized as a donor in this world. Allah would order hellfire for these three sinners.[28]

It must be noted that martyrdom, scholarship, and charity are recognized as acts of Islamic worship. In the above three cases, even if the acts of worship were performed, the intentions behind them were to obtain the approval of other humans. So Allah rewarded those people with what they aimed for – worldly recognition.

Islam expects a pristine monotheistic belief, in which both the intention and the act of worship are performed to please Allah alone and none other. Islam even defines a term for the scenario where Allah's worship is performed with the intention of worldly recognition. The Prophet^{PBUH} called it *riyaa* (show off) or 'hidden shirk (polytheism).' For example: "[If] a man [stands] up [and] prays but *lengthen* his prayer because he sees someone looking at him [so that he gets approval as a pious person]."[29] That man would do the sin of *riyaa*.

The approval of other humans has no significance because the Quran says: **"[Allah] You give honor to whomever You want and humiliate** whomever You want" (3:26). If a believer tries to impress onlookers with his/her worship, this means that s/he has incorrect concept of Allah because only Allah gives respect or humiliation.

Allah is the only Doer. Only Allah can make events occur. *Only* Allah can open our hearts and minds to see His guidance. Humans cannot do this on their own: **"Allah has created you and what you make"** (37:96), along with the input from our senses and our perception: **"As for those who *reject faith*, it is the same, whether you (O Prophet) warn them or you don't, they will not believe [Allah judged that their determination to reject faith is final]. Allah has sealed their hearts and hearing, their eyes are covered, and there is a grievous punishment for them"** (2:6–7). This subtle point reveals Islam's beauty. If you believe a human is an *independent* doer, God can no longer be the *Almighty*! Why? Because God no longer has control over the independent doers. In Islam, Allah, the Almighty, is the only Doer.

In conclusion, if a person has an unwavering intention to reject all invitations to Islamic guidance (Allah will know when the intention is final), Allah seals such a person's heart from further guidance.

IS EINSTEIN'S ARGUMENT APPLICABLE TO ISLAM?

Though Einstein's statement is logical, do not forget it is based on *human logic*, originating from a human mind. His conclusion carries an unspoken assumption: since Almighty God has total control, therefore *humans cannot be responsible for their thoughts, feelings, and actions*. In other words:

> **ILLUSION**
> Humans cannot imagine a scenario where *"God is omnipotent, and simultaneously, humans have free will."*
> Therefore, they conclude that it is also impossible for God to create such humans.

This extrapolation projects *human limitations onto God*. The reason is that Einstein's God is *imagined* by a human. Therefore, *God tacitly inherited several human constraints*. This conclusion is not surprising. Instead, it is an essential part of being human. Because, a horse will think like a horse and a lion will think like a lion (chapter 2).

The following section demonstrates that God-of-Islam is not limited by human constraints, thereby invalidating Einstein's argument in the context of Islam.

WHY ARE HUMAN LIMITATIONS <u>NOT</u> APPLICABLE TO THE GOD-OF-ISLAM?

The following points prove the uniqueness of Allah:

1. Islam is not a Xenophanic religion at all.

> In the entire Quran, there is not a single incident of anthropomorphism.

2. The Quran says:

> **"There is nothing like Him [Allah]"** (42:11)

Allah and His creation do not share *common characteristics*; therefore, in the absence of any similarity, it makes no sense to impose human physical or mental limitations on the God-of-Islam.

> **Why are Human limitations not applicable to the God-of-Islam?**
>
> The following example illustrates this point. Water covers 71% of the earth's surface. Does that mean that 71% of the sun's surface is also covered by water? This comparison has a fundamental logical flaw. That is because the sun's composition and temperature are entirely different. For example, the sun is a nuclear inferno of continuous proton-proton fusion. The sun is not a solid mass; its surface temperature is 10,300° Fahrenheit.[30] Whereas water boils at 212 degrees Fahrenheit. *If two entities are completely different from each other, don't expect them to share any common characteristics.*
>
> Can you think of *even a single similarity common between the God-of-Islam and humans?* We already discussed in chapter 2 that verse 3:7 prohibits literal interpretation of similes or allegories; otherwise, you will violate the verse: **"There is nothing similar to Him [Allah]"** (42:11).
>
> *How can God-of-Islam and humans share the same limitations and restrictions if they don't share any common characteristics?*
>
> *Nauzubillah* (it means "we seek refuge from Allah").

3. **The Quran Instructs Us: "Do Not Try to Project Human Limitations onto Allah."**

   Pagan Ubayy bin Khalaf was a fierce opponent of Islam. He took a dried bone in his hand, crushed it, and scattered its pieces in the air, then challenged the Prophet[PBUH], "O Muhammad[PBUH]! Are you claiming that Allah will resurrect this?" In response, Allah revealed verses of the Quran (36:77-83) (the verses are explained in chapter 6 of this book). The verses point out that it makes no sense for humans to deny the omnipotent power of Allah by quoting a task that is *impossible for humans*. Instead, humans should recall that Allah is the originator and creator of the earth, along with the entire universe and six other skies. It is Allah who unites a sperm and egg in the mother's womb to create a human. Then Allah nurtures the fetus all the way to child birth and continues to provide for him till s/he becomes an adult. Even then, some people doubt the existence of Allah. The verses also remind us that on the Day of

FREE WILL AND THE PREDESTINATION PARADOX

Judgment we will all be judged based on our belief. Humans should not make wild guesses or extrapolate what Allah can or cannot do. Can anyone still doubt the power of Allah to create?

> Verses (36:77-83) point out that projecting human limitations upon Allah is illogical. Therefore, such projection is prohibited.

QURAN-BASED CONCLUSION # 1
Based on verses 16:1, 42:11, and (36:77-83), the Quran proves that *human limitations do not apply to the God-of-Islam*. If a human being cannot accomplish any task, it does not mean the same is true for the God-of-Islam.

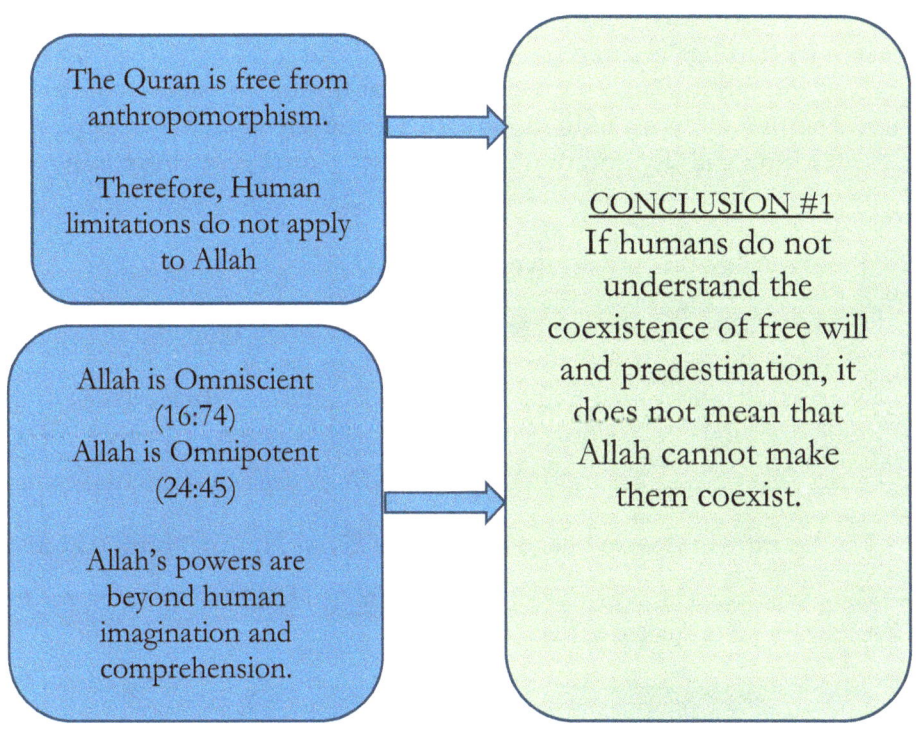

The Quran Guides: Allah is the Originator, the Creator, the Controller, and the Omnipotent

Many verses of the Quran inform us about the extraordinary creative powers of Allah. For example, the Quran says:

"**God has power over everything**" (24:45).

"**Whenever He [Allah] wills a thing, He just commands it "BE" and it is [created]**" (36: 82).

"**Allah created everything, and He is in charge of everything**" (6:102).

"**He (Allah) has created the heavens without a pillar as you can see, fixed the mountains on the earth so that it may not shake you away, and settled all types of living creatures therein. We have sent down water from the sky and made all kinds of plants grow in gracious pairs**" (31:10).

"Surely, Allah has power over *all things*" [35:1].

> **QURAN-BASED CONCLUSION # 2**
> In the true sense of the word, Allah is omnipotent. Verses 24:45, 36:82, and 6:102 prove that human mind and imagination are incapable of fully comprehending His divine abilities: "**Allah creates whatever He wills**" (24:45).

The Quran Guides: What to Think and What Not to Think About

The verse (42:11) says that there is nothing like Allah. Therefore, the following verse makes perfect sense:

"Compare none with Allah" (16:74).

That is not all. The Quran strictly prohibits anyone from making *wild guesses and extrapolations* about Allah:

FREE WILL AND THE PREDESTINATION PARADOX

> "Has Allah indeed permitted you or do you invent (ideas) to attribute to Allah?" (10:59).

Since humans have limited knowledge and Allah is beyond human imagination, *human rules, ethics, and logic do not apply to Allah*. It, therefore, makes no sense for a created being even to question, criticize, or evaluate Allah:

> "He [Allah] is accountable to none about what He does, but they [entire humanity] are accountable to Him" (21:23).

> **QURAN-BASED CONCLUSION # 3**
> Verses (16:74), (10:59) and (21:23) prohibit *comparing* anything or any entity to Allah. He is above and beyond the limits of human thinking and imagination.

The Quran Guides: Human Knowledge is Limited

The Quran tells us:
1. "**Surely Allah knows, and you do not know**" (16:74) and
2. "**No one can grasp anything from His [Allah's] knowledge besides what He has permitted them to grasp**" (2:255).
3. "**Our Lord has encompassed *all things* in knowledge**" [7:89].

Only Allah has total knowledge about everything. Humans have very limited knowledge. Some information we may learn in the future, while some information is beyond the realm of human understanding. The Quran calls such information 'hidden knowledge' or *ghaib*, which only Allah knows and no one else does. For example, only Allah knows when the Day of Judgment will occur.

> **QURAN-BASED CONCLUSION # 4**
> Every bit of human knowledge is a blessing of Allah. Only Allah has total knowledge. Humans *do not and cannot* know it all.
> Verses 16:74 and 2:255.

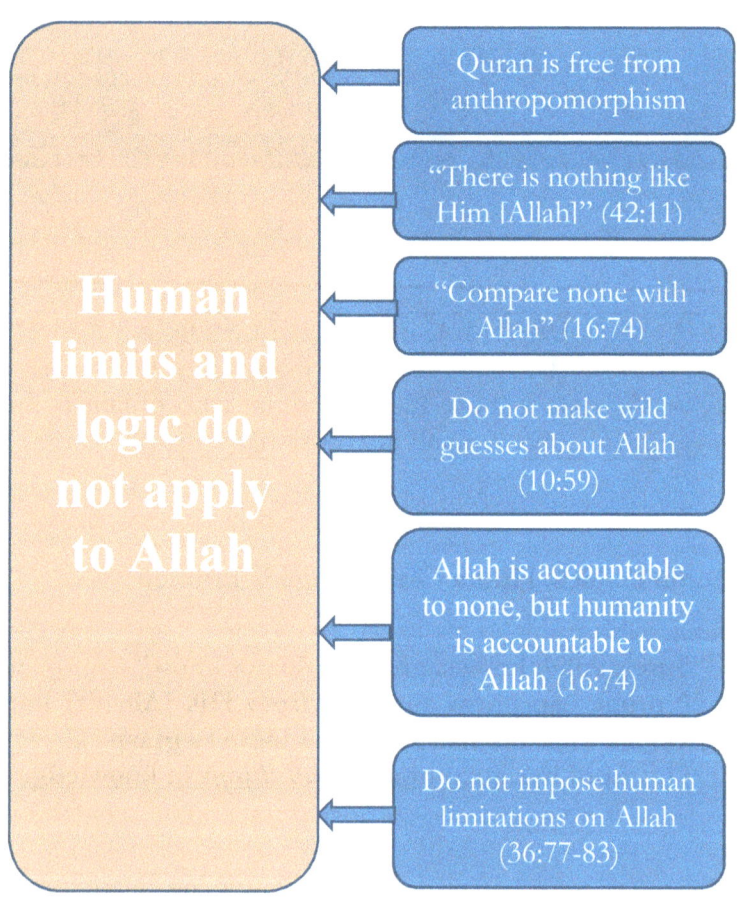

FREE WILL AND THE PREDESTINATION PARADOX

RESOLUTION OF FREE WILL AND PREDESTINATION PARADOX

The following verse makes an unusual claim that there is no contradiction in the Quran: "**Will they not ponder on the Quran? Had it not come from someone other than God, they would have certainly found therein many contradictions**" (4:82).

This verse emphasizes two important points:
 a. The verse tells us to *contemplate* the Quran to look for deeper meanings.
 b. The verse *guarantees* that Quran does not have contradiction anywhere.

> Verse (4:82), therefore, compels us to ponder and find a reasonable explanation for the apparent contradiction between verses (6:39) and (18:29).

Reconciliation Step 1 of 3
Pondering The Attributes of Allah

Let us look closely at the omniscience and omnipotent powers of Allah [Quran-based conclusion # 2 and #4]:
 a. "**Our Lord has encompassed *all things* in knowledge**" [7:89].
 b. "**Surely, Allah has power over *all things***" [35:1].

The Quran tells us that Allah made seven heavens, including the earth. The Quran does not describe much about the six heavens, but verse [37:6] tells us that the first heaven is our universe. According to verses 7:89 and 35:1 above, Allah has total knowledge of everything, and simultaneously He controls everything in the universe. This includes every lifeform and lifeless entity. It means that Allah is the only one who knows and controls the movements of every galaxy, black hole, star, planet, and moon. Allah's knowledge and control also extend and encompasses down to every subatomic particle and every photon across the universe throughout time. The minuscule amount of knowledge humans have on all subjects is only granted by the permission of Allah. The Quran precisely describes: **"Allah knows, and you [humans] do not know"** (16:74). In summary:

(1) Allah has total knowledge of present, past and future of everything throughout the universe.
(2) Human knowledge and learning capabilities are limited.

We have already proved that Islam is free of anthropomorphism therefore human limitations do not apply to Allah. He transcends all human limitations. He is above and beyond human logic and comprehension. To resolve the paradox of free will and predestination, it is imperative that we must *go beyond our conventional human thought processes*.

> **Reconciliation Step 1**
> If humans do not understand the coexistence of free will and predestination, it does not mean that Allah cannot make them coexist.

Reconciliation Step 2 of 3
Comparing Apples and Oranges

In the USA, the presidential election is held every four years. The voters are given an ample chance to *compare* the candidates and elect the most suitable contender. For example, the final two Presidential candidates debate each other. Here the two candidates share many similarities. For example, candidates meet the minimum qualifications to run, have political aspirations, and enjoy substantial voter support.

Comparison is a common logical method humans use to choose among the available alternatives. If you plan to buy a car, you will compare the available car choices in your price range. However, the comparison does not make sense if the two entities are entirely different. For example, if you are deciding which coat to wear to a party, you will not compare a coat to the black hole of the Milky way galaxy. When making decisions, it is our natural habit to compare the available options. There is also a trap:

FREE WILL AND THE PREDESTINATION PARADOX

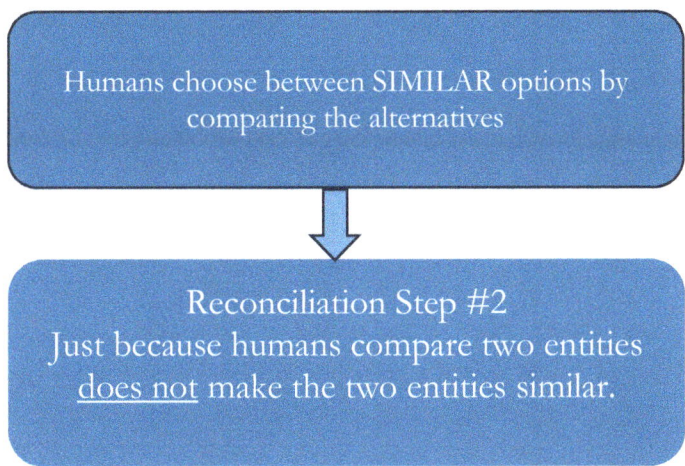

When we discuss Allah, we should avoid the old habit of comparing. Why? Because "**there is nothing like Him**" (42:11). Therefore, in the absence of any similarity, nothing can be compared to Allah. In addition, the Quran guides us to avoid this pitfall: "**Compare none with Allah**" (16:74).

Humans are unable to imagine how free will and predestination can coexist. People assume that since humans cannot imagine it, by *comparison*, God cannot imagine it either. The underlying assumption is that *humans are similar to God*.

For Xenophanic religions, it is a valid argument. But how can this argument be valid against Islam, which is free from anthropomorphism?

When the Quran says: (1) nothing is similar to Allah, and (2) nothing can be compared to Allah, there is no reason to assume that human limitations can be applied to Allah. He is an omnipotent and majestic whose power and grandeur are beyond human comprehension.

Reconciliation Step 3 of 3

The verse (18:29) says that Allah gave human the *free will*. Similarly, verse (6:39) says that Allah has *predetermined* who will be a true believer and who will go astray. *Because verse (4:82) says that there is no contradiction in Quran*, this leads to undeniable conclusion that both *verses (18:29) and (6:39), are simultaneously true and <u>do not contradict</u> each other*. In the eyes of humans, free will and predestination are incompatible, but Allah's perspective transcends this duality. *It is irrelevant whether humans can or cannot imagine such a scenario.*

> If omnipotent Allah says He can do any task, then Allah can.
>
> Human limitations do not limit Allah.

⬇

> The Quran says it contains no contradiction (4:82).
>
> This includes all predestination and free will verses.

⬇

> **RECONCILIATION SUMMARY**
> Allah made predestination and free will, so they coexist.
>
> Free will and predestination may seem incompatible from the human viewpoint, but the perspective of Allah transcends this dichotomy.

Humans have free will; therefore, Divine punishment is justified

Suppose an employee notices a possible way to steal money from the employer. In this example, it is assumed that no third party is coercing the employee. Then, the employee will have a choice (or free will) to steal or not to steal. As discussed earlier in this chapter, the employee's *intention* sets the course. Whatever the employee chooses to do, the employee will be accountable in the afterlife. The Quran emphasizes that *Allah is always just* and humans are rewarded or punished based on their own deeds in worldly life: **"Whoever acts righteously does so for his own good and whoever commits evil does so against his soul. <u>Your Lord is not unjust to His servants</u>"** (41:46).

FREE WILL AND THE PREDESTINATION PARADOX

"**This [Allah's judgment] is due to what your two hands have sent [your deeds] before, and because Allah is not in the least unjust to the servants**" (22:10).

"**God does not do even an atom's weight of injustice**" (4:40).

At the same time, Allah *predetermines* all actions, movements, and events. Nothing can go against Allah's plan. Nothing can happen unless Allah permits. All humanity is slave of Allah (chapter 2). As suggested by the proposed reconciliation, predestination does not interfere with free will.

> **RECONCILIATION SUMMARY (CONT.)**
> Allah made Free will and Predestination simultaneously true.
> Humans have free will therefore Divine punishment is justified

Why do Humans not understand the paradox?

Question: This paradox is important enough and has bothered humans for thousands of years. Why did Allah not reveal adequate information to humans to avoid confusion?

Answer: Allah tests us during our worldly life: "**We [Allah] shall test you through fear, hunger, loss of life, property, and crops. (Muhammad**^{PBUH}**); give glad news to the people who have patience**" (2:155). Chapter 4 of this book explains that *confusion* caused by a lack of knowledge is also a type of test from Allah.

How does the paradox of free will and predestination affect our beliefs? Our response to this question determines if we pass or fail Allah's test. Some people become atheists, while others remain religious.

SKEPTIC? SIMPLE ANSWERS USING QURAN AND SCIENCE

VERSES THAT ENDORSE THE PROPOSED RESOLUTION

APPARENT CONTRADICTION
1. Freewill-supporting verses: (18:29) and (41:40).
2. Predestination-supporting verses: (6:39) and (57:22).

GUIDANCE FROM THE QURAN
3. Verse (4:82) guided us to resolve the contradiction by *pondering the Quran*. To put it simply, if you want to reconcile, seek guidance from the Quran.

ALL PRAISE IS FOR ALLAH
4. Allah is omnipotent (24:45), (36: 82), (6:102), (35:1), and (31:10).
5. Allah is omniscient (16:74) and (2:255).
6. There is nothing like Allah (42:11).
7. Allah is beyond human knowledge and imagination: (16:74).
8. Compare nothing to Allah (16:74), (10:59), and (21:23).
9. Allah is never unjust to His servants (41:46).
10. Do not make wild guesses about Allah (10:59).
11. Allah is not accountable to anyone, but entire humanity is accountable to Allah (21:23).

KEYS TO THE SOLUTION
12. *Islam does not have anthropomorphism therefore, human logic and limitations cannot be applied to God-of-Islam* (42:11), (16.1), (16:74), (10:59), and (36:77-83).
13. Allah is Omniscient, while *human knowledge* is limited (16:74).
14. Verse (4:82) says that *the Quran does not have contradiction*. In this context, our *limited* human knowledge creates the illusion of contradiction.

SOLUTION
➢ Even if *it is beyond human comprehension, free will and predestination do not contradict.*
➢ Humans have free will to choose their actions; therefore, Divine punishment is justified (41:46), (22.10), and (4:40).

It is irrelevant whether humans can or cannot imagine such a scenario.

THE LOGICAL STEPS PRESENTED ABOVE ARE BASED SOLELY ON THE QURAN AND HADITH. THEY ARE NOT THE AUTHOR'S PERSONAL VIEWS.

FREE WILL AND THE PREDESTINATION PARADOX

A CHALLENGE FOR ANYONE WHO DISAGREES WITH THE PROPOSED RECONCILIATION

The proposed reconciliation of free will and predestination paradox is entirely based on the claim that Islam is free of anthropomorphism. That is why we concluded that *human logic cannot be applied to the God-of-Islam*. Those who disagree are invited to take on the following challenge:

> *In the entire Quran, find just one incident of anthropomorphism in which Allah is the same as a human. Please do not use hidden meanings or similes as discussed in (3:7), and do not contradict the Quran, as in verse (4:82).*

Point to Think About

> We cannot comprehend how free will and predestination can be compatible.
>
> However, to test us, Allah put the answer in verses and told us to ponder the Quran (4:82).

The lack of human knowledge does not indicate the absence of guidance

Once, a companion of the Prophet asked him, "Can a person give up good deeds and rely on predestination?" the Prophet[PBUH] instructed him to *continue doing the good deeds* and recited this verse: **"Who gives in charity, fears Allah, and testifies to goodness, We [Allah] shall facilitate for him the easy way"** (92:5-7)[31]. Therefore, Muslims should continue to do their best to do good deeds and maintain the right beliefs. Confusion regarding the free will and predestination paradox is no reason to relinquish domestic, religious, or social duties.

In other words, belief in predestination does not mean giving up our efforts. Once, the Prophet[PBUH] noticed a *Bedouin* (nomadic Arab) had left his camel untied. The Prophet[PBUH] asked the Bedouin: "Why don't you tie down your camel?" The Bedouin responded, "I put my trust in Allah." The Prophet said, "Tie your camel first, then put your trust in Allah."[32] Therefore, we should always put forth the best effort within our means first and only then rely on Allah's predestination.

Is "I do not know" a valid answer?

Undoubtedly, predestination and free will cannot be explained using understandable human logic. How did Allah solve the paradox? We *do not know*!

If a high school student writes "I don't know" on an examination, he or she will not receive any credit for that question. In school exams, 'I do not know' is the same as a wrong answer.

If you encounter a challenging question about Allah and cannot find the answer in the Quran and ahadith, then 'I do not know' is not only valid *but the only correct answer.*

Wrong answers or wild guesses about Allah can mislead others. The person providing the wrong information will be held accountable on the Day of Judgment. Humans have been given only limited knowledge about Allah and many other subjects. Even the Prophets did not have full knowledge. For example, Allah told the Prophet Noah, **"Do not ask me about that which *you have no knowledge*"** (11:46).

Wait for the Full Explanation

Given that human limitations do not apply to Allah, how does Islam explain the free will and predestination paradox? After all, the human mind is always curious. At some point, we would like an understandable answer, particularly if that answer involves divine punishment.

Islam only *postpones* the explanation of this paradox; Islam does not ignore it. The Creator of the universe takes it upon Himself to explain all such riddles. Allah advises believers to tell non-believers regarding their arguments and doubts: **"*Be patient* until Allah judges *between us* [on the Day of Judgment], for He is the best of all judges"** (7:87). On the Day of Judgment, Allah will settle *all* of our arguments. This includes every philosophical paradox we can imagine. It includes the free will-

FREE WILL AND THE PREDESTINATION PARADOX

predestination paradox and responsibility for horrific actions committed by humans like Ted Bundy.

During this life, a Muslim is supposed to believe in the unseen Allah, ponder Allah's signs for spiritual support, and obey Allah. When you are unsure, remember the wise words of an Urdu couplet:

> Tu dil mein to aata hi, samajh mein nahi aata
> Main jaan gaya bas teri pehchan yahi hai
>
> *Allah, I can feel You in my heart but fail to understand You*
> *Finally, I figured out how to recognize You!*

The subject of 'Anthropology of Religion' confirms that, throughout history, people have been strongly attracted to Xenophanes' versions of the divine. They prefer a human-god instead of a shapeless, formless, and idol-less God. Paganisms of ancient Greek, Egypt, Norse, and Germanic religions are good examples.

> Why has Islamic monotheism stayed so pure and pristine for over 1400 years?
> *That is something to think about!*

FOUR

WHY DOES GOD ALLOW SUFFERING? (PART 1)

Probably the most persuasive atheist argument is: "If God is merciful and benevolent, then why do evil and suffering exist?" For centuries, all over the world, people have been asking different versions of this question. The irony is that while many may be confused about the existence of a merciful God, almost every adult is certain that evil and suffering exist. In this context, following an ancient argument makes sense even today. This argument is attributed to the Greek philosopher Epicurus[33]:

> *Is God willing to prevent evil but not able?*
> *Then he is not omnipotent.*
> *Is he able but not willing? Then he is malevolent.*
> *Is he both able and willing? Then whence cometh evil?*
> *Is he neither able nor willing? Then why call him God?*

To defend their god, theists, scholars, and preachers of all religions have offered a wide range of explanations. In this context, *theodicy* is defined as an "explanation of why a perfectly good, almighty, and all-knowing God permits evil. The term [theodicy] literally means 'justifying God.' "[34]

For example, according to Greek mythology, Pandora opened a box that contained all kinds of misery and evil. Thus, evil was released to cause suffering to humans. This is one attempt at explaining why evil exists.

WHY DOES GOD ALLOW SUFFERING?

Pandora

Another example of ancient theodicy is 'Babylonian Theodicy,' a poem written about 1000 BCE in ancient Babylon. This poem consists of a dialogue between two friends who ponder suffering and the role of the divine.

"The first [friend] says that religion and cultivating his relationships with the gods seems to do nothing, and the second warns the first that it is unwise to question the greater wisdom of the gods and cosmos. The first [friend] asks how we can get out of suffering, and the second says that a good and just life is rewarded. The first says that animals and humanity commit crimes that go unpunished, and the second says that no crime truly goes unpunished."[35]

Babylon ruins, Hillah, Iraq

Islam accepts the existence of hardship and suffering. The good news is that Allah also gives humans complete guidance on how to endure life's ups and downs, including all kinds of suffering. Islam teaches us how to remain *emotionally* at peace, even when our life is overwhelmed by hardship and turmoil. Therefore, the discussion of this topic is divided into two parts. This chapter discusses Islamic theodicy. Appendix A describes 'Islam's 'hardship survival kit.'

RENAMING 'SUFFERING' AS 'TESTS OF ALLAH'

The Quran guarantees that every human will be tested:

> "We [Allah] shall test you through fear, hunger, loss of life, property, and crops. (Muhammad^{PBUH}), give glad news to the people who have patience" (2:155).

Does it make a big difference if we rename 'suffering' as 'tests of Allah'? For all practical purposes, they are one and the same. However, our choice of the name refers to how we emotionally respond to our predicaments, perceive Allah, and interpret life in general.

When one calls hardship *suffering*, it means we believe that some uncontrollable power (or bad luck) is causing us physical and emotional pain, which is likely to continue in different forms until we die. Life often feels like a never-ending battle, with brief moments of joy scattered between periods of suffering. According to Poet and Nobel Laureate Joseph Brodsky (1940-1996), "Life—the way it really is—is a battle not between good and bad, but between bad and worse."[36]

The Goal is to Guide Humanity to the Right Path

Islam provides an entirely different interpretation. Allah's tests have a distinct purpose, as explained by the following Hadith:

> Amongst My [Allah's] believing-bondsmen [worshipers] are those whose belief will not be improved except by poverty, and if I enrich them, it will be ruined. And there are amongst My believing bondsmen those whose belief will not be improved except by enriching them, and if I impoverish them, it will be ruined. And there are amongst My believing bondsmen those whose belief will not be improved except by sickness, and if I made their bodies healthy, it would have corrupted them. And there are amongst My believing bondsmen those whose belief will not be improved except by good health, and if I give them sickness, it will cause them to corruption. And I organize their affairs by My knowledge of what is in their hearts, for I am the All-Knowing.[37]

> Allah's tests have been carefully customized for each individual to benefit them in the long run.

This means Allah's trials and tests are not random. Instead, the tests are designed to serve a purpose based on an individual's abilities and circumstances.

The 'Tests of Allah' Have Constraints

These tests are tough, but Allah also promises:

> "[Allah] does not impose on any soul a responsibility beyond its ability" (2:286).

SKEPTIC? SIMPLE ANSWERS USING QURAN AND SCIENCE

It means that if the test appears too challenging, Allah gives more strength and resilience to the person being tested. Only Allah knows the details. Suffering is our challenge, and our reaction to suffering is the test. Although often not evident, we will eventually see that Allah always guides us to the right path. Allah promises Paradise to those who follow His guidance and have patience (verse 2:155 above).

Always Have Hope – Allah is Most Merciful

Along with the tests of this life, Allah gave us the continuous blessing of hope:

> "Never give up hope of Allah's mercy" (12:87)

That is because the Quran says that along with hardship, there is relief:

> "Certainly, after every difficulty, there comes relief" (94:6)

It means even if the present seems bleak, a believer should always be hopeful because Allah guarantees relief. On the Day of Judgment, the oppressed victims will be fully compensated because "**He [Allah] is the best Judge**" (6:57).

Appearances Can be Deceptive

Why does suffering exist? This question has troubled humans for thousands of years. Since the Quran is the Book of Allah, it must address such a prominent question.

It turns out that the Quran directly addresses this issue in the form of a story about Prophet Moses[PBUH]. This story tells us that Allah sent Moses[PBUH] to a wise scholar, Al-Khidr, to gain knowledge. During their time together, Al-Khidr advised Moses[PBUH] to be patient and refrain from questioning his actions unless Al-Khidr voluntarily explained. Moses[PBUH] agreed. Both went for a boat ride. Al-Khidr tore a hole in the boat. Moses[PBUH] asked Al-Khidr why he endangered the lives of the people in the boat. Al-Khidr reminded Moses[PBUH] not to question him. Moses[PBUH] apologized and promised not to ask any more questions. Both continued to travel. Al-Khidr met a boy and killed him. Again, Moses[PBUH] asked the reason for the unjustified killing, Al-Khidr reminded him not to ask any questions. They both continued to travel and reached a town. The people of the town refused to give them food. There Al-Khidr saw a wall that was about to fall. Al-Khidr fixed the wall to make it sturdy. Moses^{PBUH} told Al-Khidr that if he informed the townspeople, they might pay him for his service.

At that point, Al-Khidr told Moses^{PBUH} that he had asked too many questions and could no longer accompany Al-Khidr. However, Al-Khidr explained his actions. He tore the boat to make it defective because, down the river, a king was confiscating boats in good shape. By damaging it, Al-Khidr saved the boat from confiscation and helped its owners. The boy belonged to pious parents, but as an adult, he would become a sinner and a cruel person. Al-Khidr killed the boy to save his parents from suffering. Allah may bless parents with more children. Underneath the wall, the deceased parents of two orphans buried a treasure. Al-Khidr made the wall sturdy so the two orphans, who lived in that town, could find the treasure when they grew up. Al-Khidr said that every action was a command from Allah and not his own ideas (18:65–82).

Let us analyze this story. When Al-Khidr damaged the boat, it was a loss of property. When he killed the boy, it was a loss of life. In both scenarios, the long-term goal was to assist deserving individuals, even if the reasoning behind it was not initially apparent. In the third case, Allah's help came, while the beneficiaries (the orphans) were unaware of it. In all cases, Allah is helping and guiding us, but sometimes we are unable to appreciate it because our knowledge is limited. This story also teaches us how humans should react when they face the loss of property or life. *We should be patient*, even if we can only see the partial picture. Being patient was not easy even for Moses^{PBUH} because he kept asking for the justification for Al-Khidr's actions. But patience and trust in Allah are the only solutions. The Quran repeatedly says that Allah knows it all, while humans have incomplete knowledge. Our suffering may be a blessing in disguise. As the Quran says, "**You may *not like something* which, in fact, *is for your good* and something that you *may love,* in fact, *maybe evil*. God knows, but you do not know**" (2:216).

Confusion is Part of Allah's Test
In the above story, Moses^{PBUH} did not endure any physical hardship or suffer any loss of property. However, his test was about *how he reacted to the confusion of having incomplete information.*

SKEPTIC? SIMPLE ANSWERS USING QURAN AND SCIENCE

We are no exceptions. We are also bound to face confusing situations because Allah made some knowledge beyond human intellect. So how should we react to such confusion? The answer is also found in the following verse, which is part of the above story.

Before starting the journey, Al-Khidr told Moses[PBUH], "**indeed, with me, you will never be able to *have patience*. And *how can you have patience for what you do not know?***" (18:67-68). In other words, one must be patient *even if one lacks knowledge*. We should *avoid* quick and impulsive decisions. Instead, have patience and *continue to believe in Allah*. After all, so many signs prove that Allah exists.

> Just because confusion exists in some areas is not a reason to abandon your faith in Allah.

Questions

During the Battle of Uhud, there was a rumor that the Prophet[PBUH] had been martyred. Some Muslims became disheartened, but others held on to their beliefs steadfastly. In the face of adversity, Allah tested the companions by observing how they handled confusion and uncertainty. We must have strong faith to remain firm in the face of challenges.

> **Allah's Tests Open the Door to Our Spiritual Growth**
>
> Rumi said, "These pains you feel are messengers. Listen to them." No doubt, some tests change our thinking and personality. During our suffering, deep inside, we become aware of our human limitations and helplessness. This experience may make some people atheists, and some remain unaffected.
>
> Nonetheless, some of us will make genuine spiritual progress. Our introspection makes us realize that only Allah has control and only He can provide relief. For example, once Prophet Moses^{PBUH} felt utterly helpless, he prayed from the depths of his heart to Allah, **"O Lord! Surely I am in desperate need of whatever good that You may send down to me"** (28:24). Similarly, Prophet Zakariyah^{PBUH} felt the vulnerability of his old age and prayed **"O Lord! Surely my bones have weakened and the hair of my head glistens with gray, …. grant me an heir by Your grace"** (19:4–5). In times of emotional and physical distress, our prayers to Allah are sincere and genuine, leading to spiritual growth.
>
> Can you recall any incident when personal hardship guided you toward spiritual growth?

CONCLUSION

Allah tells us that humans will be tested or undergo some hardships. However, the challenges are carefully tailored to an individual's resilience and endurance. Allah made some people poor because Allah knew if they were rich, they would be ruined. Allah ensures that no person is burdened beyond his/her ability to endure. Allah also assures us that along with difficulty, we also get relief. The challenges or Allah's test we face in this life may have long-term benefits, even if we are unaware. Also, the trials of Allah may open the door to spiritual growth.

> **BUT THIS IS ONLY A PARTIAL PICTURE**
>
> If a book on Islamic theodicy only discusses life's challenges without recognizing Allah's guidance as a source of comfort, it does not effectively convey the divine message. This can lead to a distorted understanding.

APPENDIX A contains Allah's guidance to overcome "emotional suffering" in a very short time. In the absence of emotional suffering, we are better equipped to respond to worldly challenges. We learn how to live a peaceful life despite challenges and hardships. No doubt Allah is **"The Most Beneficent, the Most Merciful"** (1:3)

FIVE

THE WATCHMAKER ANALOGY

This subject has interested philosophers like Aristotle and Plato[38] but was recently made famous as the *watchmaker analogy* by the English clergyman William Paley (1743–1805). Paley pointed out that if he finds a perfectly working watch on the ground, then "the watch must have had a maker-that there must have existed, at some time and at some place or other, an artificer or artificers who formed it for the purpose which we find it actually to answer, who comprehended its construction and designed its use."[39]

> ### THE PARADOX PRESENTED BY THE WATCHMAKER ANALOGY
>
> Simply put, the watchmaker analogy implies that a watch that works flawlessly is evidence that it was not created by a random event such as an earthquake, hurricane, flood, tsunami, or meteor shower. A watch that moves its hand precisely every second and accurately tracks every minute must have been carefully *designed* by a watchmaker. Also, the existence of the watch proves that it was created for the purpose of calculating time. In other words, *if the watch exists, its designer must also exist*. Our universe is far more complex and precise than a watch; the planets and stars move and rotate at precise speeds. Therefore,
>
> *The existence of the universe proves that its ultimate designer (God) also exists.*

Atheists may respond, "If the above argument is correct, then who designed the designer?" In other words, if the existence of the universe proves the existence of God, then by the same token, the existence of God proves that God also has a creator! Richard Dawkins and Jerry Coyne, who are considered strong proponents of the theory of evolution, said, "If complex organisms demand an explanation, so does a complex designer. And it's no solution to raise the theologian's plea that God (or the Intelligent Designer) is simply immune to the normal demands of scientific explanation."[40] Is this argument correct?

For all Xenophanic religions, the atheist's argument is perfectly valid. Since God is a man, he must eat, or he will become hungry. He must drink water to quench his thirst. If he is wounded, he will bleed. How can anyone claim that God is a man if he has none of these limitations? In other words, a human-god is *bound by human logic* and limitations, though a human-god may also possess some godly traits.

According to the above argument, not just a watch but every object has a creator. Therefore, human-god, who is bound by human logic, must also have a Creator!

IS THE QUESTION "WHO DESIGNED THE DESIGNER" APPLICABLE TO THE GOD-OF-ISLAM?

This is not a new question. By referring to God's ancestry, desert dwellers asked the Prophet[PBUH] the same question, and Allah answered them

THE WATCHMAKER ANALOGY

(chapter 2): **"He [Allah] begets not, nor is He begotten"** (112:3). This unusual concept has no parallel with earthly lifeforms. Throughout the Quran, Allah remains unique in every way. For example, today, there are more than eight billion people on earth, while **"Allah is one"** (112:1). In contrast to humans, **"Allah is Self-Sufficient"** (112:2). There is no concept of self-sufficiency among humans. For example, humans depend on air to breathe and gravity to keep them grounded on Earth.

The atheist's question, "Who designed the designer?" is based on human logic that is inapplicable and incompatible with Allah. Why? Because, in Islam, the Creator never becomes part of His creation, and the creation never becomes part of the Creator. So there is no overlap between man and God. Please recall the example of the Earth and the Sun (chapter 3). The Creator never shared any trait or property with His creation. The Quran is very clear: *"there is nothing like Him [Allah]"* (42:11).

> Allah is pure and free from all human limitations or anthropomorphic associations.

Claiming that human logic is also applicable to Allah is trying to impose human characteristics and limitations on the Creator of humanity. That is not possible in Islam. The Quran says, *"compare none with Allah"* (16:74) and **"there is nothing like Him [Allah]"** (42:11). We discussed this subject in chapters 2 and 3.

In Islam, even imagining a similarity between Allah and humans is considered *shirk* or polytheism, which is a major sin: **"He [Allah] is far above and beyond from the *shirk* (polytheism) they do"** (16:1).

THE QURAN RESPONDS TO ANOTHER OBJECTION

The atheist may object, "What is the proof that God, as defined in verse **"He [Allah] begets not, nor is He begotten"** (112:3), exists?" If we reject the message in verse 112:3, we must admit we are *only guessing* because there is no parallel to Allah in our worldly experience. No scientific evidence can prove that the above verse 112:3 is not true.

The following verse of the Quran responds to the above objection and asks a profound question:

SKEPTIC? SIMPLE ANSWERS USING QURAN AND SCIENCE

> The Quran prohibits people from making wild guesses. **"So far you have been arguing about things of which you had some knowledge! Must you now argue about that of which you know *nothing at all*? Allah knows while you do not"** (3:66).

A Challenge to Atheists

The arguments used in this chapter to prove that God-of-Islam does not have a creator are based on the rationale that *Islam is entirely free from anthropomorphism*. In case, you disagree, with this claim, our previous challenge to find any evidence of anthropomorphism in the Quran is applicable again:

1. Can you find any verse in the Quran that proves that Islam is an anthropomorphic religion or that human logic binds Allah? (Please do not use *hidden* meanings or similes, and do not contradict any verse of the Quran, including verse 42:11). Once again, the Quran challenges: **"Produce proof to your claim, if you are truthful"** (2:111).
2. The Quran asks you: **"Do you attribute to Allah something which <u>you do not know</u>?"** (2:80).

Atheism contains some major logical weaknesses. It cannot prove that God does not exist. Atheists do not explain how matter, time, and energy originated out of *nothing*. According to atheist ideology, the universe is created and sustained by chance. In other words, without any help from God. Based on these assumptions, atheists conclude that God does not exist. The Quran points to the weakness in this approach: **"The fact is that most of them [the unbelievers] follow nothing but mere wild guesses, and guess cannot be a substitute for the truth"** (10:36).

Islam, however, has the answer to how the universe originated. The Quran says Allah created seven heavens, including our universe, as quoted in verse 31:10 (chapter 3). The Quran says, **"All power belongs to Allah"** (2:165). Therefore, Allah created all the forces of nature, including gravity, magnetism, and electricity. Allah also created the laws of science.

THE WATCHMAKER ANALOGY

Was *Darkness* Created?

Some religions say God created light. The Quran gives an entirely new perspective by saying, **"Praise be to Allah ... [who] made the *darkness* and the light"** (6:1). This verse tells us that Allah created not only the light but also *darkness*. Even cave dwellers knew that in the darkness of night, during a lightning storm, they could momentarily see their surroundings, but as soon as the lightning stopped, darkness reappeared. We assume that when light is absent, darkness is a natural and inevitable outcome. According to the above verse, even darkness did not exist by itself. Allah created darkness, along with the light.

> *"What was it like before Allah created light and darkness?"*
> No wild guesses, please. Instead, justify your answer with scientific evidence.

While answering the above question, keep in mind that Islam rejects the ideology that *all matter in the entire universe, including light and darkness, is God* (Pantheism). In Islam, any part of Allah's creation (including all matter) is NOT God. That is why idols cannot be divine in Islam, and their worship is prohibited. The Quran also says, **"there is nothing like Him [Allah]"** (42:11).

> Verse 6:1 says Allah *created* light and darkness. Therefore, neither light nor darkness can be God.

Some people claim that a man authored the Quran. Humans cannot even imagine what it was like before darkness and light were created. Nonetheless, the Quran mentions an impossible concept far beyond human imagination.

> *Can atheists guess who authored the above Quranic verse (6:1)?*

THE QURANIC VERSION OF 'THE WATCHMAKER ANALOGY'

According to the atheists' response to the watchmaker analogy, God should also have a creator. They suggest that the existence of God is illogical. In contrast, the Quran asks similar questions that *promote thinking in the right direction*.

Verse 52:35 of the Quran asks the following *three* questions. Each question builds on the previous question. The first two questions are about humans. We relate well to humans, so we can easily answer them. The third is about the entire universe, including every lifeform and lifeless object. Here is the first question:

> "Were they [the humans] created without a Creator?" (52:35)

A Muslim will answer no to this question because the Quran says that **"He [Allah] created man"** (16:4). A non-Muslim theist will also answer no to this question, even if their definition of Creator differs from Muslims'.

An atheist or evolutionist might say that humans were created by a long evolutionary chain. Humans or *Homo sapiens* was the last link, whereas the first link (or origin of life) was some bacteria-like micro-organisms. But how life originated remains unknown or is credited to some mysterious chemical reaction. In other words, some mysterious event was the creator. Therefore, the answer to the Quranic question is still no.

The second question is:

> "Or were they their own creators?" (52:35)

It is highly unlikely that any Muslim, non-Muslim theist or atheist would claim they gave birth to themselves. Again, the unanimous response to this question would be no. The third and last question is:

THE WATCHMAKER ANALOGY

> **"Did they create the Heavens and the Earth?" (52:36)**

Again, no person is likely to argue that s/he is the creator of the universe. Remember that you are also part of the universe. If you could not create yourself, how could you create the universe? The unanimous answer to this question is again no.

After saying no three times in a sequence, a person becomes aware of human limitations. These verses inspire the logical mind to reflect on life's origin and the role of the creator. If some chemicals created life as bacteria-like micro-organisms in the ocean, who created the chemicals? Who created scientific laws that allow chemical reactions to generate life? Who created the ocean? Who created the earth? How was space and time were created? Who created the universe? Was the universe created without a creator or by itself? We agreed earlier that a man cannot create himself, and a woman cannot create herself. Everything has a creator. How could the universe exist without a creator? So, who created the universe? The Quran answers: **"It is Allah, Who created the Heavens (including our universe) and the Earth"** (14:32).

The above three questions are more relevant today than ever before. Science has already established that the universe did not exist since eternity. Instead, the universe began after the 'big bang.' But that couldn't have happened without a Creator. So, we can say with certainty that Allah is the Creator of the universe.

As discussed above, you cannot continue to say 'who created God' because the Quran says: **"He [Allah] begets not, nor is He begotten"** (112:3). The Quran is free from all types of anthropomorphism, and Allah is not bound by human logic in *any way*. Therefore, the verse **"He [Allah] begets not, nor is He begotten"** (112:3) is true even if humans cannot understand how.

CONCLUSION
The above discussion logically proves that atheists' arguments against the watchmaker analogy do not apply to the God-of-Islam. This shows the timeless beauty of the Quran and that it can easily refute atheists' arguments even in the 21st century.

The Quran rejects all types of direct and indirect anthropomorphism. The Quran does not contain contradictions. There is so much depth and originality in these concepts that the human mind cannot easily comprehend them. Humans are incapable of inventing such far-reaching original ideas. No doubt, the Quran is the book of Allah.

SIX

THE OMNIPOTENCE QUESTION

WHAT IS THE OMNIPOTENCE QUESTION?

Can God create an immovable stone that even God cannot move? For centuries, different variations of the omnipotent questions have been puzzling the believers of all religions. These questions may seem like harmless jokes, but they have the potential to impact an individual's faith in God. They suggest that the concept of God is logically impossible; therefore, God cannot exist. Theist scholars have provided a range of answers to such questions. For example, Ibn Rushd (1138-1198 CE) discussed various versions of omnipotent question.[41] Recently, Steven Hawkins referred to this issue in his famous book 'A Brief History of Time.'[42] To this day, the omnipotence question remains a mystery.

SKEPTIC? SIMPLE ANSWERS USING QURAN AND SCIENCE

Ibn Rushd

SOME VARIATIONS OF THE OMNIPOTENCE QUESTION
Conflict with other attributes of God: "Can the Omnipotent God kill Himself?" Similarly, "Can the Omnipotent God discontinue the attribute of All Seeing?" **Conflict with God's nature**: Once, I was discussing Islam with a non-Muslim friend. I said that the beauty of Islam is that 'God never

converts into a man.' My point was that Islam was not created or tempered by humans, otherwise, anthropomorphism would have been inherent. My friend responded, 'in my religion, God is Omnipotent, and He can convert into a man!' How does one respond to this argument? Here is another example: "Can God create another God just like Himself?"

ANALYZING THE IMMOVABLE STONE QUESTION

The following example can help us understand the stone question.

Note: An integer is a whole number (not a fraction). Therefore, the numbers 98, 729, 10002, 8, and -55 are all integers.

Consider the three questions below:
1. Please identify an *even* integer between 1 and 10. The correct answer will be any number from 2, 4, 6, 8, or 10.
2. Please identify an *odd* integer between 1 and 10. The correct answer will be any number from 1, 3, 5, 7, and 9.
3. Please identify an integer between 1 and 10, which is both *even and odd*.

The last question cannot be answered. Why? Because, by definition, an integer can be either even or odd. It can never be both. The last question has two contradictory or mutually exclusive conditions; therefore, *it cannot be answered*. Such questions have an inherent flaw that makes them invalid.

Similarly, the stone question has two contradictory conditions: (1) God created an immovable stone. (2) God is Omnipotent; therefore, God can move everything. This question, as well, contains an inherent flaw. *It is, therefore, an invalid question.*

The above logic makes sense for humans. But a person can still ask, 'the stone question has two mutually exclusive conditions *for humans*, but what about the Omnipotent God, who is capable of doing everything? *Do human limitations also constrain God?*' This problem will be discussed later in this chapter.

SKEPTIC? SIMPLE ANSWERS USING QURAN AND SCIENCE

WHEN THE PROPHET FACED THE OMNIPOTENCE QUESTION

We discussed in chapter 3 the incident of Ubayy bin Khalaf who crushed a dried bone and asked the Prophet[PBUH] if Allah could bring it back. In response, Allah revealed the following verses of the Quran. Let us study the verses in detail:

"Does man not see that We [Allah] created him of a <u>sperm-drop</u>, and lo! he is flagrantly <u>contentious</u>" (36: 77)?

"He presents for Us a <u>similitude</u> and forgets his own creation. He says: 'Who will give life to these bones when they have rotted away and became dust' " (36: 78)?

"Say (O Prophet Muhammad[PBUH]), 'He who created them <u>in the first place</u> will give them life again: He has full knowledge of every act of creation" (36: 79).

"It is He who produces fire for you out of the green tree – lo and behold!– and from this, you kindle fire [Arabs used to rub branch of Markh tree and the `Afar tree to generate fire[43]]" (36: 80).

"Is He who created the <u>heavens and earth</u> not able to create the likes of these people? Of course He is! He is the All-Knowing Creator" (36: 81).

"Whenever He wills a thing, He just <u>commands it "BE,"</u> and it is [created]" (36: 82).

"So glory be to Him in whose Hand lies <u>control over everything</u>. It is to Him that you will all be <u>brought back</u> [to life to be judged and sent to paradise or hell]" (36: 83).

The above verses contain many arguments regarding the omnipotence question.

(36:77): Allah gives life and death not just to humans but to all life forms. Allah gives life to every individual cell in every plant and every animal. This includes every sperm and every egg. *At the stage of a sperm, humans are completely helpless*, and obviously at the mercy of Allah. However, after Allah nurtures and blesses humans with the ability to walk, talk and think, some

THE OMNIPOTENCE QUESTION

humans arrogantly imagine themselves as invulnerable. They begin to argue and doubt the omnipotence of their own creator.

(36:78): The verse points out that it makes no sense for humans to deny Allah's omnipotence by quoting a task that is impossible for other *humans*. True, no human can recreate a crushed, scattered, powered dry bone back into its original form because the human ability is limited. But how come the same human limitation is applicable to Allah? Think about it. This issue was discussed in the context of Quran-based conclusion # 1 (chapter 3).

(36:79): The verse reminds us that originally, Allah gave life to all humans. Humans do not have the ability to give life to themselves or anything else. The verse points out that Allah is also omniscient.

(36:80): This verse is self-explanatory.

(36:81): Allah created seven heavens and the earth, not just humans. Think about the size of the universe along with all its complexities. Besides, there are six more heavens. How can you doubt Allah's ability to create? Allah is omnipotent and omniscient.

(36:82): When a human tries to make something (say a ballpoint pen), they go through several stages: accumulating resources and raw materials; acquiring the know-how accumulated by others; practicing the manufacturing process; failures; learning from past experience; improvements and retries; gradually improving the product; and finally making an acceptable new product. Next, humans restart this entire cycle to create an improved version of the same product. For humans, the manufacturing process takes a great deal of effort, time, and careful consideration. Allah simply said BE, and the universe began with the big bang. It has been going through stages exactly as Allah planned. How can anyone doubt the omnipotent ability of Allah? Let us remind ourselves that humans cannot effortlessly create anything. While Allah effortlessly created the entire universe out of *nothing*.

(36:83): This verse contains a subtle warning that a time will come when Allah will judge humans and award them heaven or hell. Put simply, it's crucial for humans to acknowledge their total dependence on Allah. No doubt, Allah is omnipotent. Denying any attribute of Allah is a sin.

SKEPTIC? SIMPLE ANSWERS USING QURAN AND SCIENCE

> **EVEN PHILOSOPHICAL QUESTIONS MUST FOLLOW SOME CONSTRAINTS**
>
> Suppose you want to find a weakness in arithmetic. You will have to find a conflict among the existing rules/formulas of arithmetic. You cannot object to a single isolated arithmetic formula without proving the conflict with another formula. For example, according to arithmetic, 2 + 2 = 4. Here you cannot say that 'arithmetic has a weakness because it cannot make 2 + 2 = 5.' Similarly, you cannot say, 'why cannot arithmetic drop the multiplication operation?'

GUIDANCE FROM THE QURAN

The omnipotence question is a significant dilemma that has survived for many centuries. On the other hand, the Quran is Allah's Book; therefore, it must contain the answer to this question. And it does. The Quran provides *helpful rules to guide believers*. To respond to the omnipotence question, some verses from the Quran are summarized below. Like the above example about the arithmetic rules, any challenge-questions directed at Islam should not violate the fundamentals of the Quran, and must observe the following rules/constraints:

Constraint #1: Do not contradict the Quran

In verse 4:82, the Quran states that it contains no contradiction. When a question challenges Islam, it should not be expected that Allah would contradict any part of the Quran! Otherwise, the basic principle of non-contradiction would be violated. For example, the Quran says that one of Allah's attributes is All-Seeing. Consequently, the omnipotence question cannot challenge God to drop the attribute of All-Seeing. Similarly, the Quran says there is only one God. Therefore, no question can challenge God to create more than one God.

Constraint #2: Do Not Equate Incompatible Entities

The Quran and ahadith have declared that some entities are unequal. For example:

Say (O Prophet Muhammad[PBUH]**): "Not equal are Al-Khabîth (all that is evil and bad as regards things, deeds, beliefs, persons, and**

foods) and <u>At-Tayyib</u> (all that is good), even though the abundance of Al-Khabîth may attract you." (5:100)[44]. So the question cannot be asked, 'can the omnipotent God make evil and good equal?' That would contradict the verse (5:100).

Similarly, as restricted by the following verse, a challenge question cannot be asked to make an obedient believer of Allah equal to a disobedient person: **"Then is one who was a believer like one who was defiantly disobedient? They are not equal"** (32:18).

Constraint #3: Do not make wild guesses about Allah.

Allah is way beyond human imagination. For that reason, the Quran strongly prohibits anyone from making wild guesses about Allah (10:59). This condition also applies to the challenge-questions directed at Islam.

Constraint #4: Do Not Assign Imaginary Attributes to Allah

We are not allowed to assign imaginary attributes to Allah: **"Has Allah indeed permitted you or do you invent [ideas] to attribute to Allah?"** (10:59).

Constraint #5: Do Not Imagine That Allah is Similar to Any Part of His Creation

The Quran says. ***"There is nothing like Him"*** (42:11). This verse cannot be contradicted.

Constraint #6: Allah's Nature Cannot Change

The Quran describes many capabilities of Allah. For instance, Allah makes a person rich or poor (42:12); He sends rain and makes people age with time (40:67); and Allah gives life and death (57:2). A challenge about God's Omnipotent capability should not expect Allah to change His Divine nature. For example, stop giving life and death.

Constraint #7: A Person Should Sincerely Seek Knowledge. The Question Should Not Be Used as a Joke to Ridicule Any Religion.

Allah warns those who ridicule Islam or Allah's message: **"When he [a misguided person] learns about some of Our [Allah's] revelations, he mocks them. Such people will suffer a humiliating torment"**

(45:9). Islam encourages humans to ponder and make spiritual progress. Only in a sincere and calm environment can a person appreciate the beauty of Islam. When people ridicule religion, spiritual progress is hindered.

Constraint #8: Human logic and limitations do not apply to Allah
We discussed this subject in chapter 3.

> Please note that every 'Constraint' above is based on Quranic verses.
> **These are not the ideas of the author of this book.**

RESPONSE TO QUESTIONS ABOUT OMNIPOTENCE

Let us start with the question: "Can the Omnipotent God kill Himself?" "Can the Omnipotent God discontinue His attribute of All Seeing?" "Can God create another God like Himself?"

We will try to answer these questions based on the above Quran-based constraints. The above questions are intended to change Allah's attributes (Constraint #4) along with His nature (Constraint #6). For example, all the attributes of Allah from the Quran and ahadith, like *Al-Hayy* (Ever-Living), *Al-Baseer* (All-Seeing), and *Al-Wahid* (One-and-Only), cannot be changed or violated. It is just like asking why 2 plus 2 is not equal to 5. Therefore, such questions are invalid.

Next, let us revisit: 'Why can't God create an immovable stone?' Please recall the example of an 'even and odd integer.' Such *self-contradictory* problems merely give the illusion of being genuine problems. They are only sentences that *look like* problems; there is no real problem. It would be a mistake to let such thoughts influence your belief in God.

This leads to a fascinating point. The Quran says, **"He [Allah] has power over all things"** (24:45). Therefore, why can't Allah do *self-contradictory tasks*?

Answer: *Only Allah knows* the details of His omnipotence. We do not know if He can or cannot do self-contradictory scenarios. We are not allowed to

THE OMNIPOTENCE QUESTION

make wild guesses about Allah (10:59), because humans have limited knowledge (16:74). Besides, human logic does not apply to Allah. To find the answer to this, we will have to wait until the Day of Judgment. Then Allah will settle all of our mutual arguments. The Quran says: **"Be patient until Allah judges between us [on the Day of Judgment], for He is the best of all judges"** (7:87).

WHY CAN'T THE GOD-OF-ISLAM CONVERT INTO A HUMAN BEING?

This question contradicts many Quran verses, like **"there is nothing like Him"** (42:11) and **"Subhan-Allah"** (16:1). Human limitations do not bind the God-of-Islam. For example, the God-of-Islam was always alive. The God of Islam never dies, while humans are born, and they die. The human body is divided into 12 anatomical systems (chapter 3). Humans have many mental, physical, and emotional weaknesses and vulnerabilities. If God became a man, He would be subject to human limitations, which would be impossible. This question directly or indirectly violates constraints # 1,2,4,5,6, and 8.

The question, "Why can't the God-of-Islam convert into a man?" is another example of Xenophanes' temptation to worship God as a human. After all, the human mind is constrained by our limited imagination. Anthropomorphism appears to be the path of least resistance. It leads to a counter-question: "Why can't you worship a God who is *not* human?"

To worship the God-of-Islam, a believer needs special spiritual maturity. If we seek, we will find that the ability to worship unseen and unimaginable Allah is already embedded in our consciousness. Finding the ability to worship an *unseen Allah* is worth the effort.

Omnipotence is a centuries-old unsolvable puzzle. Isn't it surprising that the verses of the Quran have answers to this and other questions?

SEVEN

THE THEORY OF EVOLUTION

The theory of evolution is of special interest because it involves two independent sources of information about the origin of man: science and the story of Adam and Eve from the three Abrahamic religions.

> **THE THEORY OF EVOLUTION**
> According to the Encyclopedia Britannica, all plants and animals are descendants of bacteria-like micro-organisms that originated on our planet more than 3 billion years ago.[45]
> In other words, "various types of plants, animals, and other living things have their origin in other pre-existing types. The distinguishable differences are due to modifications in successive generations."[46] This modification process is called evolution. "In biology, evolution is the change in the inherited traits of a population from generation to generation."[47]
> The theory of evolution is supported by a wide variety of scientific disciplines, including molecular biology, biochemistry, physiology, ecology, animal behavior (ethology), paleontology, geology, genetics, and others. Many of these fields were invented years after Darwin's theory was proposed. For example, Darwin died in 1882, while molecular biology as a subject emerged in the 1930s[48]. These scientific fields provide ample independent proof in favor of the theory of evolution.
> According to evolution theory, humans are no exception. Humans also evolved from other species.

THE THEORY OF EVOLUTION

Charles Darwin

On the other hand, the three Abrahamic religions maintain that Adam and Eve did not evolve from other species. They were the first human couple who started the human race.

TWO TYPES OF EVOLUTION

Some evolutions are prolonged processes. For example, a land-based hyena-like amphibious animal Sinonyx underwent several transitional forms and ended up as the modern humpback whale. Here two points are significant: the change from Sinonyx to humpback whale did not happen overnight. It took 60 million years,[49] and if we compare the two species, the change is drastic. This is an example of macro-evolution.

In some cases, evolution can be much faster. In just a few days, infection-causing bacteria can evolve and become antibiotic-resistant. That is why, when a doctor prescribes an antibiotic, they instruct you to finish all doses, even if your symptoms disappear sooner. If every dose is not taken, some bacteria from the disease may survive in the patient's body and can evolve to develop immunity to the antibiotic medication. If the patient becomes sick again with the same illness, the same antibiotic will become ineffective. This is an example of micro or small-scale evolution.

Evolution abstract illustration

EVOLUTION AS PROTECTION FROM THREATS

Animals and plants evolve to evade predators and other threats. In the 1950s, Bernard Kettlewell, a research fellow at Oxford University, discovered that "moths are changing to a darker color. The reason was the soot and pollution from industrialization made it easier for black moths to blend in with their newly dirty surroundings, while white moths were less able to blend in and more vulnerable to predation by birds."[50] In another example, for centuries, poachers have been killing elephants for their tusks. Now tuskless elephants are emerging.[51]

INTER-SPECIES RELATIONSHIPS

The above discussion proves that evolution is not an isolated activity. Instead, animals and plants try to compete, survive and preserve their species. As generations pass, predators influence the evolution of their prey, while preys affect their predators' evolution.

Brian Richmond, Curator of Human Origins at the American Museum of Natural History in New York, said, "All life on Earth is connected and related to each other."[52]

THE THEORY OF EVOLUTION

EVOLUTION DEPENDS ON RANDOM MUTATION

How does science explain the cause of evolution? Authors Ker Than, Tom Garner, Ashley P. Taylor described the cause of evolution as, "the physical and behavioral changes that make natural selection possible happen at the level of DNA and genes within the gametes, the sperm or egg cells through which parents pass on genetic material to their offspring. Such changes are called mutations."[53] According to Briana Pobiner, an anthropologist and educator at the National Museum of Natural History in Washington, DC, "Mutations are basically the raw material on which evolution acts."[54]

Mutations can be caused by random errors in DNA replication or repair or by chemical or radiation damage (ultraviolet radiation from the sun or X-rays). Most of the time, mutations are either harmful or neutral, but in rare instances, a mutation might prove beneficial to the organism. In that case, it will become more prevalent in the next generation and spread throughout the population.[55]

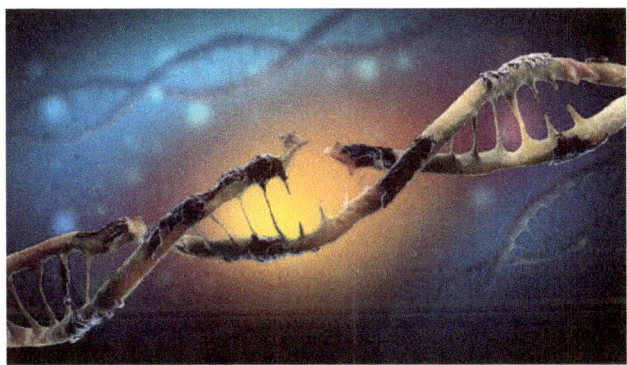

Damaged DNA

In this way, natural selection guides the evolutionary process, preserving and adding up the beneficial mutations and rejecting the bad ones. According to Pobiner, "Mutations are random, but selection ... is not random."[56]

SKEPTIC? SIMPLE ANSWERS USING QURAN AND SCIENCE

> ## HUMAN EVOLUTION
> According to the theory of evolution, who were the ancestors of modern humans or *Homo sapiens*? If we list the evolutionary hierarchy (from the earliest to the most recent), we will find:
> "Australopithecus afarensis (origin 3.2 million years ago), Homo habilis (origin 2.5 million years ago), Homo erectus (origin 1.8 million years ago), Homo Neanderthals (origin 230,000 years ago), Homo sapiens (origin about 195,000 years ago)"[57].
> In the above hierarchy, except for *Homo sapiens*, all members of the human evolutionary ladder are now extinct.

CAN SCIENCE EVER CONFLICT WITH THE QURAN?

Abu Walid Mohammad Ibn Rushd (Averroes, 1138-1198 CE) was a versatile Andalusian genius and jurist. He wrote on many subjects, including philosophy, theology, medicine, astronomy, physics, psychology, mathematics, Islamic jurisprudence, and linguistics. One of his most profound statements will remain forever valid: "Truth [revelation] *cannot contradict* wisdom [philosophy or science]; on the contrary, they must agree with each other and support each other."[58] By *truth* Ibn Rushd meant the Quran and ahadith. According to Nidhal Guessoum, Professor of Physics and Astronomy at the American University of Sharjah, UAE, "By *philosophy*, Ibn Rushd means the conclusions that Reason can reach by careful methods (or Science)."[59] In other words, the Quran and Science can never contradict each other. Let us look at the rationale behind his statement.

The Quran is the word of Allah. It is also protected by Allah because: **"We [Allah] have without doubt sent down the Message [the Quran], and We will assuredly guard it [from corruption]"** (15:9). That is why, over time, the text of the Quran has not changed. Every word of the Quran remains true.

Humans do not learn scientific knowledge on their own. Instead, the knowledge of science is given to humans by Allah's permission: **"They [humans] cannot gain access to anything out of His [Allah's] knowledge except what He pleases"** (2:255). This verse states that Allah *allows* humans to acquire knowledge. However, Allah also sets *limits* on what humans can learn. Some information we may learn in the future, while some information is beyond human understanding (*ghaib*).

THE THEORY OF EVOLUTION

When discussing the Quran and science, we essentially discuss the 'word of God' and the 'work of God.' Obviously, there should never be any conflict between the two. What a beautiful conclusion by Ibn Rushd!

> **WHAT IF WE FIND AN UNRESOLVABLE CONFLICT BETWEEN SCIENCE AND THE QURAN?**
>
> We may encounter a situation where science irreconcilably conflicts with the Quran. Instead of rejecting one or the other, we have the following options:
> 1. Sometimes a scientific observation can be wrong. Usually, the error of observation is detected over time, and scientists correct themselves. For example, between the 2nd and 16th centuries, the geocentric model of earth, which held the belief that the sun, moon, and stars revolved around the earth, was widely accepted.[60]
> 2. The verse conflicting with science could be a mutashabihat verse or a simile. In chapter 2, we discussed that **"no one knows the hidden meanings [of a mutashabihat verse] except Allah"** (3:7). In that case, the conflict with science is only symbolic and not an actual conflict.
> 3. A third option is to admit that we 'do not know' the answer or "Allah knows best." Human knowledge is limited. Only Allah has complete knowledge. 'I do not know' is a valid answer, as discussed in chapter 3. On the Day of Judgment, Allah will settle all our mutual arguments: **"Be patient until Allah judges between us [on the Day of Judgment], for He is the best of all judges"** (7:87).
>
> In the meantime, we should never reject science because Allah encourages us to acquire beneficial knowledge. A prayer in the Quran says, **"O Lord! Increase my knowledge"** (20:114). Confusing situations are tests from Allah. A Muslim should remain patient and keep acquiring beneficial knowledge, which is a gift from Allah. Beneficial knowledge should never be rejected. Instead, we should learn, benefit, teach others, and thank Allah.

SKEPTIC? SIMPLE ANSWERS USING QURAN AND SCIENCE

EXAMPLES WHERE ISLAM AND SCIENCE ARE IN AGREEMENT

Age of Planet Earth

According to Abrahamic religions other than Islam, the world is only a few thousand years old.[61] But the theory of evolution claims that life evolved from micro-organisms more than 3 billion years ago. What does Islam say about the earth's age?

How Long is the *Yaum* (Day)?

In verse 11:65, the Quran uses the plural of the Arabic word *yaum* (day) for our regular day of 24 hours. But the Quran sometimes uses the same word to indicate different time durations. For example, the following verse defines the length of one day in hellfire as **"one day [Arabic word yaum used here] for God is equal to a thousand years for you"** (22:47). Similarly, the travel time to Heaven is described in **"The angels and the Rûh [Gabriel] ascend to Him in a Day [word yaum used here] the measure of which is fifty thousand years"** (70:4). These verses prove that the Quran uses the same word yaum (day) as a homonym for different time periods. It is not always a Xenophanic version of a day on earth. After all, the earth is not the only planet created and sustained by Allah. Instead, Allah is **"the Lord of [all of the] Worlds"** (1:2).

The Quran also tells us, **"Indeed your Lord is Allah, Who created the heavens and the earth in six days [plural of word *yaum* used here]"** (7:54). As discussed above, the word yaum can indicate different time durations in different situations. Verse 7:54 does not specify exactly how long the six days were in terms of earth time. All this knowledge is part of *ghaaib* or hidden. **"No one in the Heavens or the Earth has *the knowledge of the unseen* except Allah"** (27:65). Similarly, we do not know when the fifth day ended and the sixth day started.

The Quran does not specify the age of the earth. So the statement that life evolved from micro-organisms more than 3 billion years ago does not conflict with any statement in the Quran. And regarding *how* the universe was created, Islam is in full agreement with science (explained below).

THE THEORY OF EVOLUTION

The Big Bang

The Quran describes the creation of the earth: "**Have not those who disbelieve known that the heavens and the earth were joined together as one united piece, then We [Allah] parted them?**" (21:30).

About 1400 years ago, the above verse predicted that the universe did not exist since eternity. Today we know that the universe was started by an explosion called the 'Big Bang.' In 1964, two young scientists, Arno Penzias, and Robert Wilson, were awarded the Nobel Prize for providing proof of the Big Bang Theory.[62] Therefore, the Quran is in agreement with science on this issue.

Deep Space

The Expansion of the Universe and the Creation of the Galaxies

After the Big Bang, the matter continued to expand at an amazing speed. According to the National Center of Biotechnology Information (NCBI) USA, while expanding, the matter started collecting together in bunches. That eventually created galaxies: "As the universe _expanded_, according to current scientific understanding, matter collected into clouds that began to condense and rotate, forming the forerunners of galaxies. Within galaxies, including our own Milky Way galaxy, changes in pressure caused _gas and dust_ to form distinct clouds."[63] The above quote describes that: (1) since the big bang, the universe has been expanding, and (2) some matter accumulated like clouds that eventually created the galaxies.

> The Quran also describes the expansion of the universe, **"The heavens, We [Allah] have built them with power. And verily, We are <u>expanding</u> it"** (51:47).

The Quran also talks about the consolidation of matter that eventually created the galaxies: **"Then He [Allah] established His dominance over the heaven when it was <u>smoke</u>, and said to it and to the earth: "Come both of you willingly or unwillingly." They both said: "We come, willingly""** (41:11). In the above quote, NCBI used the term 'gas and dust' to describe matter after the big bang. While the quote from the Quran used the term 'smoke.' Indeed, these are close descriptions.

Evolution of all Species Other than Human

A paper by Sean Jordan, Postdoctoral Research Associate at UCL, claims life originated in water at the bottom of the ocean.[64] From that point on, life evolved, generating new species, like fungi, protists, fishes, non-vertebrates, plants, amphibians, reptiles, mammals, and so on. If we exclude humans from this list, does the concept of evolution conflict with Islam? The answer is: not at all. That is because the Quran never claims that all species of plants and animals were created instantly. According to Hussein al-Jisr, a Lebanese Muslim scholar, "There is no evidence in the Qur'an to suggest whether all species, each of which exists by the grace of God, were created all at once or gradually."[65]

The above paper by Jodan suggests that life originated in water. The Quran also says, **"God has created every living being from water"** (24:45). Once again, this verse is supported by scientific evidence.

EVOLUTION-RELATED CONCEPTS IN ISLAM

Nothing is Random. Allah Creates All Incidents/Events

All evolution can be attributed to mutations at the level of DNA and genes. As discussed earlier, according to science, mutations are entirely random and influenced by many unpredictable events.

However, according to Islam, Allah plans every event, and absolutely nothing is random. Therefore, we can conclude that Allah intended to give

THE THEORY OF EVOLUTION

life forms the ability to evolve. That means Allah created the processes of mutation and evolution. He created dinosaurs and put some at the top of the food chain for a limited period. Allah also planned to make them extinct at a specific time. So, all life forms continued to evolve precisely as Allah intended.

Allah's Prior Plan to Send Adam and Eve to Earth

Even before Adam and Eve *were created*, Allah planned that humankind would inhabit the earth: **"Your Lord said to the angels: "Verily, I am going to place [mankind] generations after generations <u>on earth</u>.""** (2:30). This proves that neither sin nor the arrival of Adam and Eve on earth was *an unexpected event*. Allah knew the future of Adam and Eve. Also, Allah did not plan that Adam and Eve would live in paradise forever.

How did the earth look when Adam and Eve were sent to inhabit it? Certainly, the earth did not look like the moon's or Mars' surfaces, where there is no water, vegetation, or life form that can be used as food.

Instead, Allah made the earth habitable for humans. Before sending Adam and Eve to earth, Allah told them, **"there will be for you on earth a *habitation and provision* for a while"** (7:24). To make the earth habitable for humans, Allah created vegetation, animals, and other lifeforms, so humans could use them as food and for other needs. The vegetation and animals that humans consume as food also depend on other lifeforms to live on. For example, Allah created grass so sheep can survive and small bugs and seeds so chickens can eat. The Quran says, **"There is no living creature on earth that does not receive sustenance from Allah"** (11:6). The entire environment of various food chains was created so humans could survive generation after generation. **"It is He [Allah] who has made the earth subservient to you [humans]. You walk through its vast valleys and eat of its sustenance"** (67:15).

> This leads to a significant conclusion: when Adam and Eve came, the earth was already populated *with different life forms and evolution was already in progress.*

> **RELATIONSHIP BETWEEN ISLAM AND SCIENCE**
>
> There is only one divinity in Islam, which is Allah. He is omnipotent. If electrons revolve around the atomic nuclei, then it is because Allah ordered them.
>
> Besides matter, Allah also made the laws of science. Allah has revealed some laws of science to humans so they can benefit from them. These laws include methods to generate electricity and how to develop medicines to cure different diseases.
>
> Science is not interested in any religion or God. Therefore, the *concept* that 'God is the only doer' is not part of science. This statement, however, does not mean that there is a conflict between Islam and science because the statement that 'Allah is the only doer' does not conflict with any scientific *law* or *fact*. Instead, according to Islam, Allah enforces the laws of science, and He is the doer who created all events.

ORIGIN OF HUMANS: TWO OPTIONS

Option 'A': The Origin of Humans according to Evolutionary Theory

About 195,000 years ago, *Homo sapiens* evolved from Homo Neanderthals. Humans did not evolve from the currently living species of chimpanzees or bonobos. However, humans and contemporary chimpanzees shared a common ancestor that lived between 5 and 8 million years ago. According to the American Museum of Natural History website, "The chimpanzee and bonobo are humans' closest living relatives... These three species look alike in many ways, both in body and behavior ... Humans and chimps share a surprising 98.8 percent of their DNA."[66] The DNA similarity between humans and chimpanzees and many other scientific pieces of evidence prove that, like other lifeforms, Homo sapiens also evolved from Homo Neanderthals.

Option 'B': Proposed Reconciliation with Islamic Values

Life originated in water exactly when and where Allah wanted it. With the exception of Homo sapiens, all lifeforms on earth went through evolution, as supported by science. Allah created chimpanzees and bonobos about 5 to 8 million years ago, with DNA similar to humans. According to the independent scholar Glen Moran "(Yasir) Qadhi (an American Muslim theologian) sees no problem in accepting evolution so long as this does not include human beings."[67]

According to Islam, Adam and Eve were the first human couple. They did not evolve from another species. *Homo sapiens descended from Adam and Eve.*

Our proposed reconciliation aims to avoid any conflict between the 'word of God' (the Quran) and the 'work of God' (study of Allah's creation or science). To reconcile, we must answer the following:

Question: How do we explain the scientific evidence that supports the evolution of *Homo sapiens* from Homo Neanderthals. If humans did not evolve, why is human DNA similar to chimpanzees?

Answer: Allah is the only God, therefore that only Allah can cause events to occur. No human can do anything, no incident can occur, and no scientific law can work unless Allah allows it. Every single event that has happened or is happening now is only by the will of Allah. Whatever will happen in the future can take place only with Allah's permission. Therefore, every evolutionary step of all life forms throughout time occurred precisely when, where, and how Allah wished. The verses **"We [Allah] caused human to remain as a drop of sperm in [the wombs] firm keeping. We made that drop into a clinging form, and We made that form into a lump of flesh, and We made that lump into bones, and We clothed those bones with flesh, and later We made him into other forms—glory be to God, the best of creators** [23:13-14]" describe that Allah is the controller of every stage of human embryo development, which includes DNA mutation at the time of conception.

This means that all the evidence supporting humans' evolution was created with Allah's permission. Specifically:

1. All scientific evidence found in Homo Neanderthals that proves they are the *ancestors* of Homo sapiens was created with Allah's permission.
2. On the other hand, all evidence found in Homo sapiens that proves they are *descendants* of Homo Neanderthals was also created with Allah's permission.

SKEPTIC? SIMPLE ANSWERS USING QURAN AND SCIENCE

But, as an exception, Homo sapiens did not evolve from any animal. That is because, unlike other evolving species, Allah *prevented* humans from evolving from Homo Neanderthals. Instead, when the time was right, Adam and Eve were sent down to earth as the first human couple. That was what Allah planned.

Question: *Why did Allah create such evidence that humans evolved from Homo Neanderthals?* For example, the gradual progression of DNA modification.

Answer: The Quran *guarantees* that humans will be tested during their worldly life:

> "Do people think they will not be tested because they say, 'we believe'?" We had certainly tried those who lived before them to make sure who was truthful in their faith and who were liars." (29:2-3).

For a test to be valid, there must be some degree of doubt and a lack of information. For that reason, in this life, humans cannot see heaven, hell, angels, or Allah. If we could have just a glimpse of hell while we are alive, all our doubts about Allah's punishment would be permanently removed. At that moment, every single person would instantaneously convert to Islam. There would have been no need for any Prophet to preach Islam and try to convert people.

The Quran says: **"Had your Lord willed, the whole of mankind would have believed in Him"** (10:99). This means Allah does not *force* Islam on humans. Instead, Allah gave humans religious guidance, partial information (in some areas), and free will (chapter 3). The decision to accept or reject Islam ultimately lies with each individual.

Only with Allah's permission can there be a conflict between the theory of evolution and the story of Adam and Eve. Our reaction to this confusion is the test from Allah (the role of confusion as a 'test from Allah' was discussed in chapter 4). This type of test is very similar to the confusion among Muslims during the battle of Uhud when it was rumored that the Prophet[PBUH] had been martyred. Some Muslims became disheartened, but others held on to their beliefs steadfastly (chapter 4).

THE THEORY OF EVOLUTION

When going through such spiritual tests, it is essential to reflect, gain knowledge, and consciously decide to worship Allah without any ambiguity. The Quran instructs Muslims, **"Do not be among the doubters"** (10:94). It is true that humans lack knowledge in some areas. However, with our intellect and Allah's guidance, we have an adequate background to make the right decisions.

Here is an example of 'confusion as a test.' Prophet Moses[PBUH] was a member of the Israelites, who were enslaved by the Pharoah. Prophet Moses[PBUH] conveyed Allah's message along with His miracles to Pharoah and his people. In this incident, Allah did not make Moses[PBUH] a powerful king. If Moses[PBUH] were a mighty king, his job of preaching Islam and freeing the children of Israel would have been trivially simple. By the same token, if there were scientific proof of the existence of Adam and Eve, there would have been no confusion. Both scenarios are tests from Allah. By making Moses[PBUH] one of the oppressed Israelites, Allah's message did not come from a person of authority and power. His listeners had only one option: to evaluate Allah's message on its own merit. This created confusion in the audience. If one had accepted Allah's message, it would have meant acknowledging that Allah chose a slave of Pharoah, rather than the powerful Pharoah himself, to fulfill the duties of a Prophet. Further, the Egyptian ruling class would have to obey the orders of an enslaved person to free the children of Israel. This was not an easy decision because Pharoah and his leaders enjoyed an overwhelming dominance over the enslaved Israelites. The difficult tradeoff influenced the decision of the Egyptian ruling class. Out of arrogance, they chose supremacy over the Israelites and ignored Allah's signs: **"We [Allah] sent Moses and Aaron with Our miracles to Pharoah and his people. But, these people also proved to be *arrogant*"** (10:75).

The Pharoah and his people ignored that only Allah could give wealth and status. Even after they witnessed numerous miracles of Allah, they continued to reject His message and failed the test: **"They will be exposed to the fire in the mornings and the evenings, and on the Day of Judgment, they will be told, "the people of Pharoah, suffer the most severe torment"** " (40:46).

As we benefit from various branches of science, we begin to believe that our knowledge is the result of our wisdom, dedication, and ingenuity throughout generations. Therefore, we have made so many discoveries to make our lives more comfortable and healthier. We have also become rich and arrogant. We forget that only Allah can give us knowledge, comfort, wealth, and health. Such arrogance is based on the following illusion:

> **ILLUSION**
> Our belief in or disbelief in God determines whether or not God exists.

In response to the above illusion, please recall the Hadith that quotes an example of needle and thread to describe Allah's infinite grandeur and majesty (chapter 1, verse 2).

The theory of evolution forces us to choose a side. Like the Pharoah and his people, we also face a difficult tradeoff when we try to answer the question: *how did humans originate?*

Most of us will encounter various forms of tests from Allah throughout our lives. The following incidents tell us how Allah's tests profoundly influence lives:

HOW DID THE PROPHET[PBUH] RESPOND TO THE CONFUSION OF INSECURITY AND UNCERTAINTY?

In the early phase of his prophethood, Prophet Muhammad[PBUH] started to preach Islam to the people of Mecca. He was exceptionally dedicated and sincere, and his sermons were highly effective. People from all walks of life began to convert to Islam. The introduction of Islam as a new religion posed a challenge to the traditional pagan beliefs of Mecca, which were followed by the overwhelming majority of its citizens. Additionally, they viewed Islam as a threat to their social, family, and economic frameworks.

To contain Islam, the pagans relentlessly oppressed the converts, and the Prophet[PBUH]. Imagine the pressure on the Prophet[PBUH], who was trying to protect the new Muslims, while he himself was a target of insults, ridicule, and physical attacks. A pagan leader once hit the Prophet[PBUH] so hard that his head bled.

Muslims who were poor or slaves without tribal protection suffered the most. Slave Yasir and his wife, Sumayya, suffered terrible torture. They were repeatedly forced to lie on the burning hot sand and severely beaten. Their Muslim son Ammar was at times tossed up on

> burning coals. Eventually, Yasir and Sumayya died, but they refused to renounce Islam. Another slave, Bilal, was mercilessly tortured: "Sometimes a rope was put around his neck, and street boys were made to drag him through the streets and even across the hillocks of Makkah. At times he was subjected to prolonged deprivation of food and drink; at others he was bound up, made to lie down on the burning sand and under the crushing burden of heavy stones."[68] Still, Bilal refused to recant Islam. A slave woman, "Zinnira was beaten so harshly that she lost her eyesight.[69]" Other enslaved women, Lubaina, Nadia, and Umm Umais, were mercilessly tortured. Slave Khabbab bin Al-Aratt, "experienced exemplary torture and maltreatment. The Makkan polytheists used to pull his hair and twist his neck and made him lie on burning coal with a big rock on his chest to prevent him from escaping."[70] *None of them renounced Islam.* Many victims of torture requested the Prophet[PBUH] to find a way to end the ongoing oppression. At that time, the Prophet[PBUH] could only preach patience and pray to Allah. Throughout this time, he was unable to provide a practical solution to all Muslims in Mecca.
>
> After a lot of effort, the Prophet[PBUH] managed to find a new home for Muslims in the city of Medina. Then, he ordered Muslims to migrate there, and, in the end, he himself migrated to Medina. The persecution in Mecca lasted nine long years, and throughout this ordeal, *no one knew when or if it would end.* Imagine the uncertainty the Prophet[PBUH] faced. Nonetheless,
> 1. *Throughout the ordeal, he remained patient.* The Quran praises patience in several verses: **"seek comfort in patience and prayer. Allah is truly with those who are patient"** (2:153).
> 2. Despite the confusion of uncertainty, his belief in Allah remained firm and unwavering.

In the context of the evolution theory, we lack scientific evidence that Adam and Eve were the first human couple (similar to how the Quran predicted the Big Bang). During this state of confusion and uncertainty, just like our Prophet, we should continue to have patience and full faith in Allah and pray, **"My Lord, grant me more knowledge"** (20:114).

ISLAM GUIDES: HOW TO PASS ALLAH'S TESTS

True, Allah created a test for us in the form of an unproven story about Adam and Eve. The good news is that Allah has also given us guidance on how to pass such tests.

SKEPTIC? SIMPLE ANSWERS USING QURAN AND SCIENCE

1. Reflecting on Allah's Signs to Strengthen Your Faith

The Quran includes many signs and miracles that help us remain firm in our beliefs during times of confusion and hardships. For example, in chapter 5 of this book, we discussed that Allah not only created light but also *darkness*. This concept is entirely beyond the realm of human imagination and scientific discoveries. No human can imagine how it was before Allah created light and darkness. It is a clear sign that the Quran is the book of Allah.

When we reflect on the signs or miracles of Allah, usually we only think of miracles like parting the sea by prophet Moses[PBUH] or turning a staff into a snake. But the Quran wants us to ponder everyday events like changing nights and days and regard them as signs of Allah to strengthen our faith (see verse 13:4 in chapter 2 of this book).

2. Do Not Give Up Your Faith

Even if we are facing confusion and lack knowledge, we should remember that we are being tested and never lose faith in Allah. We do not want to fail Allah's tests. After all, as in the above example, in the early phase of Islam, Muslims did not give up their faith even if the pagans from Mecca were mercilessly torturing them.

3. How to Resolve Disagreements When You Only Have Partial Knowledge?

The Quran describes a story of a group of Muslim youths trying to escape persecution by a pagan society. They hid in a cave and prayed to Allah for help. Allah blessed them with guidance and made them sleep for some three centuries. When Allah awakened them, society was no longer persecuting Muslims. There was confusion among the youth's as to how long they had slept in the cave. There was a difference of opinion. But they quickly settled the argument by saying, "**your Lord knows better how long we have stayed here [in the cave]**" (18:19).

When we have limited knowledge, sometimes prolonged arguments are counterproductive. Just say, "Allah knows best." This answer can also be applied to confusion regarding the theory of evolution and Islam.

THE THEORY OF EVOLUTION

Please recall the relevant subjects discussed under the following subheadings of chapter 3:

- Is "I do not know" a valid answer?
- Wait for the Full Explanation

DOES ONE *NEED SCIENTIFIC PROOF* TO BELIEVE IN ALLAH?

The remainder of this chapter offers additional points in support of the story of Adam and Eve.

The Quran says: **"Soon We [Allah] will show them [the humans] Our signs in the *Universe* and in *their own souls*, until it becomes clear to them that this [Quran] is indeed the truth"** (41:53). We discussed several scientific miracles of the Quran as signs of Allah in the universe. But, according to the above verse, there is an additional dimension that can guide us to make the right decision: *signs of Allah in our own souls*. Here are some examples:

No Scientific Proof Needed: Personal Spiritual Experiences

Have you ever had a personal experience that has made you believe in Allah? Did you ever feel Allah's love? Have you ever heard an inner voice saying, 'God is one?' When you were in extreme desperation or lost a loved one, did Allah help you recover? Have you ever unexpectedly heard a verse of the Quran that guided you to make the right decision?

> If you have had a moment of enlightenment that has strengthened your faith, you do not require additional scientific evidence to validate it.

That experience will always remind you that Islam is the true religion. What a beautiful hint from verse 41:53 to look into our souls.

No scientific proof needed: Peace through Islamic Worship Rituals

Engaging in Islamic worship rituals can be a profoundly fulfilling and tranquil experience, especially when making a Hajj pilgrimage, loving

Allah, reading the Quran, and donating to charity. Daily supplications (*salah*) are an excellent opportunity to relieve stress and connect with Allah several times a day. There are some special moments when you can feel Allah in your heart with more certainty than in your own existence.

No scientific proof needed: Natural Inclination to worship Allah

The Quran tells us that before any human was put on Earth, Allah created the souls of all humans and made a covenant: **"Allah asked them [all human souls]: '*Am I not your Lord [Supreme God]?*' They all replied: '*Yes! We bear witness that You are.*' This We [Allah] did, lest you humankind should say on the Day of Resurrection: 'We were not aware of this fact that You are our Lord and that there will be a Day of Judgment' "**(7:172).

Why do we not remember this promise to Allah? Because the choices between right and wrong we make in this life are tests by Allah. To make the tests valid, some knowledge is hidden from us. However, true Muslims **" believe in the unseen [Allah]"** (2:3).

Nonetheless, this covenant remains hidden somewhere in our subconscious. On the Day of Judgment, Allah will give us some additional knowledge we do not know during our earthly lives. The last sentence of the above verse (7:172) tells us that, on the Day of Judgment, all humans would acknowledge that they had an adequate recollection of the covenant during their lifetimes. Therefore, we are accountable for our choices.

Because of this natural inclination, even today, Islam is the fastest-growing religion on earth.[71] This also explains the spread of Islam among Australian aboriginal peoples[72] and Latin Americans.[73]

Here is a question for the reader: do you feel a natural inclination toward Islam?

No scientific Proof needed: Loving Allah and Feeling His Love
Something amazing happens when a person sincerely follows Islam with proper understanding: deep inside, s/he feels peace and tranquility. One discovers that Islam nurtures, grows, develops, flourishes, and prospers in love, and only love, and nothing else but Allah's pure and continuous unconditional love. Medieval Islamic jurisconsult and theologian Ibn Qayyum explains love as "the very spirit of Islam, the pivotal point of religion and the axis of [eternal] happiness and deliverance"[74] It is literally impossible to imagine spiritual Islam without love.

THE THEORY OF EVOLUTION

> Once [Sufi] Rabia Basri was asked, "Do you love Allah?"
> She answered yes.
> "Do you hate the devil?"
> She answered, "My love for Allah leaves me no time to hate the devil."[75]

Rabia's love for Allah was uninterrupted, unconditional, beautiful, and infinite. *Love engulfed every moment of her existence.* Loving Allah takes a believer to the highest form of spiritual ecstasy. On the other hand, hating anyone causes suffering to one's own self. Rabia had no reason to take time away from everlasting bliss to hate the devil. Those who can feel Allah's love and love Allah unconditionally do not need scientific proof.

No scientific proof needed: Appreciating the Purity of Islamic Monotheism

Despite humans' irresistible attraction to anthropomorphism, even after 1400 years, Islam maintained a pristine form of monotheism. Allah is unlike anything from the human imagination or Allah's creation (chapter 2, see heading "Uniqueness of Islamic Monotheism").

TIME TO CONCLUDE

Another piece of advice from the Quran: "**People, the promise of Allah is true. Let not the worldly life deceive you**" (35:5).

Now you can respond to the question:

How did humans originate?

Recommended Reading

A significant segment of this book contains excerpts from the author's previous book, *The Purest Monotheism: Monotheistic Islam. Polytheistic Muslims* (available at: www.amazon.com/dp/B079KDYGH5), written after 19 years of rigorous study and introspection. That book contained too much information in condensed form, and many readers found it difficult to absorb. Based on their feedback, the author split his previous book into three digestible segments and published them as independent books.

Chapters 1 to 5 and 8: ***The Greatest Miracle of the Quran: Islamic Monotheism***

Chapters 6 and 7: ***ISLAM: Path of Infinite Love***

Chapters 7, 9 to 13: **An** *Islam Inspired Solution to Radicalism: A Peaceful and Practical Approach*.

A Note from the Author

Hopefully, this message finds you enjoying the subtle beauty of Islamic monotheism, which also resolves many paradoxes and doubts. Such insight facilitates spiritual growth.

Please share your thoughts about my book by writing a review. Your perspective, insights, and reactions are essential in shaping the journey for future readers and for me to grow as a writer.

Writing a review doesn't require a literary masterpiece. A few sentences expressing what you loved, what stayed with you, or how the book made you feel can make all the difference.

Here is a link to Amazon's book page: https://www.amazon.com/dp/1735740969. Thanks for your support and feedback.

With sincere appreciation,

Eeshat Ansari

APPENDIX - A

ISLAMIC WAY OF RESPONDING TO HARDSHIPS (CHAPTER 4, PART 2)

In the chapter "WHY DOES GOD ALLOW SUFFERING? (CHAPTER 4, PART 1)", we discussed how Allah tests humankind through challenges and difficulties. At the same time, Allah, the most benevolent, also teaches us how to overcome hardships *emotionally*. The teachings of Allah encompass all life experiences, from everyday stress to major setbacks.

A person who follows Allah's advice can keep his/her composure and overcome negative emotions like depression, hopelessness, loneliness, anger, fear, guilt, and others. Once liberated from the emotional burden, the person has full cognitive and physical potential available at his/her disposal. Such a person is better equipped to face worldly problems. In addition, the ability to control negative emotions strengthens the faith of a Muslim. Allah may reward those who follow His guidelines: "**He [Allah] might try you, which of you is the best in deeds**" (11:7).

Here is an example of mental control over negative emotions: immediately after the battle of Uhud, when the Prophet^{PBUH}, along with the Muslim army, reached Hamra al-Asad. They were tired, and many Muslims were wounded. At that time, Muslims received a message that a large pagan army was approaching to attack the Prophet^{PBUH} and the Muslims. Usually, such a message would have been very frightening and demoralizing. Instead, the Muslims' morale and willingness to defend Islam *increased*. This is an example of sustained emotional stability and resilience. Allah praised the reaction of the Muslims: "**The righteous and pious of those who have pledged obedience to God and the Messenger, after injury had befallen them, will receive a great reward. Such people, when warned to fear those who are gathered against them, are strengthened in their faith and say, 'God is All-sufficient as our Guardian'** " (3:172, 3:173). Later, Muslims found out that the news of an attacking pagan army was false.

In this chapter, we will overview the methodology Allah has given humankind to achieve emotional stability and peace of mind, even while facing the hardships of life.

Islam Teaches Unconditional Love

Can we continue to love someone even when they do *not* meet our expectations? Islam teaches that we must love others continuously, regardless of how they behave toward us. A good example is a mother's love for her newborn. This love does not diminish, even if the baby cries or keeps the mother awake at night.

A desert Arab came to meet Prophet Muhammad[PBUH] in Al-Masjid an-Nabawi, regarded as the second-holiest Mosque in Islam. When the desert Arab felt the need, he started urinating in one corner of the mosque. Prophet's companions tried to stop him, but Prophet Muhammad[PBUH] told them to let the desert Arab finish.

Later, very lovingly, Prophet Muhammad[PBUH] said to him, "These mosques are not the places meant for urine and filth, but are only for the remembrance of Allah, prayer and the recitation of the Quran."[76] Later, the area was washed clean with water. This incident is one beautiful example of unconditional love. Prophet Muhammad[PBUH] did not order punishment, even if it may have been justified. He did not verbally humiliate the desert Arab either.

At the same time, unconditional love does not mean you grin and bear it all or refrain from saying your side of the story. Prophet Muhammad[PBUH] tactfully and lovingly conveyed exactly what he wanted to say. This shows that unconditional love can be practiced in real life. Here we must note that the Prophet also explained *why* the mosque's sanctity must be preserved. His response was calm and logical.

In addition, loving unconditionally does not mean living in a make-believe world. What if someone crosses all reasonable limits of ethics or, without any justification, physically attacks you? In such a case, Islam allows defensive measures. In extreme circumstances, even Prophets have prayed against their oppressors, as in the case of Prophet Noah (26:117-118).

APPENDIX - A

Highest Form of Love: Loving Allah and at the Same Time Feeling Allah's Love

The highest form of love is *unconditionally loving Allah and simultaneously feeling His love.* Allah *forgives* and loves us because a verse says: **"He [Allah] is the *Forgiving*, the *Loving*"** (85:14). One of the attributes of Allah is *the Loving*. Muslims are supposed to have *maximum* unconditional love for Allah: **"those with faith have maximum love for Allah"** (2:165). Rumi said, "whenever we manage to love without expectations, calculations, negotiations, we are indeed in heaven."[77] Some Sufis have achieved the ideal state of love where a person *continuously* loves Allah and feels His love. This is a state of uninterrupted bliss, ecstasy, and contentment. Rumi said, "Wherever you are and whatever you do, be in love."

Rumi

AVOID OPPRESSION AND INJUSTICE

Islamic teachings are not limited only to spiritual and emotional aspects. Additionally, Islam teaches *practical ethics* to individuals and societies. For instance, Islam teaches Muslims to avoid oppression and injustice in all circumstances.

If individuals do not hurt or oppress one another, societal suffering will diminish. Islam promotes the following two guidelines, leading to the same goal:

1. The Quran encourages *adl* (justice), along with its synonyms [*insaaf*] (fairness) and *qist* (righteousness).[78]

2. The same idea is reinforced by repeatedly discouraging/prohibiting *zulm* (oppression and injustice). The Quran also

prohibits actions described by several close synonyms of *zulm*, including "*baghy* (encroachment, abuse), *djawr* (oppression), [*fisq*] (moral deficiency), *inhiraf* (deviation), *mayl* (inclination), and *tughyan* (tyranny)."[79]

The nearest translation of the Arabic word *zulm* is *exceeding the appropriate limits of behavior in dealing with others, while violating their essential human rights*[80] or *putting a thing in a place not its own*.[81] Any harmful/senseless action or concept is *zulm*. So, the word *zulm* encompasses the meanings of English words oppression, tyranny, and injustice.[82]

The antonym of *zulm* is *adl*. By prohibiting *zulm* and simultaneously mandating *adl*, the Quran strongly prohibits all forms of human rights violations and promotes justice. Even committing injustice/oppression on one's own self is also zulm.

One way to evaluate the importance of a concept in the Quran is to do a word count. The Quran emphasizes justice by using the word *adl* 18 times (if the word *adl* is used in a different meaning, then it is not counted here), and condemns oppression by using the word *zulm* an extraordinary 291 times (not counting occurrences of the same root word *z-l-m*, which means "darkness"). As per Brill's Encyclopedia, the concept of zulm holds profound significance in the Quran: "It can be seen as one of the most important negative value-words in the sacred book."[83] Here are some examples from the Quran:

> **Those who misappropriate the property of orphans with *zulm* [unjustly] swallow but fire into their bellies** (4:10).
>
> **Allah does not love those who do *zulm*** (3: 57).
>
> **Hellfire shall be their home, and evil is the home of those who do *zulm*** (3:151)

Zulm is man-made suffering inflicted on others. Allah says in Hadith Nawawi [# 24], "O My servants, I have made oppression unlawful for Me and unlawful for you, so do not commit oppression against one another." Allah does not do zulm on humans, "**God has not done injustice to them [humans], but they have wronged themselves**" (9:70).

APPENDIX - A

Islamic Principle of 'Live and Let Live'

Here is the Islamic version of the 'golden rule': "**do no *zulm* and you will not be subjected to *zulm*"** (2:279). If people follow this rule, they will avoid doing zulm on others and, in turn, make their own lives easier.

SUBSET OF SITUATIONS WHERE ZULM IS PROHIBITED

Zulm of Racial Prejudice

Pagan Arabs used to look down upon blacks from neighboring Africa as an inferior race. Far ahead of his time, the Prophet[PBUH] permanently prohibited racial prejudice in Islam.

Abu Dhar and Bilal were companions of the Prophet[PBUH]. Once, Abu Dharr referred to Bilal as a son of a black woman. This was considered an insult because Bilal was black. When Muhammad[PBUH] learned about this incident, he said that Abu Dharr still had the weaknesses of the pre-Islamic days of ignorance. In other words, he had not learned the Islamic teaching to avoid all racial prejudices. As a result, Abu Dharr profoundly apologized for his mistake and requested Bilal to forgive him. The Prophet[PBUH] said, "I, Muhammad[PBUH] am equally the son of a black woman as I am of a white woman." That statement made sense because, when an infant, Muhammad[PBUH] was nursed by a black woman. Only a person entirely free from racial prejudice can make such a public statement about himself. The Prophet[PBUH] also gave a beautiful message: a woman's milk gives life to the baby, regardless of her skin color. The Prophet[PBUH] treated all people as equal, and he successfully changed the thinking of Muslims, even when the concept of racial equality was totally beyond the culture of his era. Compare this to racial prejudice as practiced in many countries even today.

Zulm Against Children

Islam teaches parents to be fair to all children and not to mistreat or do zulm to less favored children. Once, a man planned to give a gift from his wealth to his favorite child while ignoring the rest of his children. He requested the Prophet[PBUH] to witness the gift. The Prophet[PBUH] asked: "Did you offer the same to all your children?" The man replied, "No!" Prophet refused to be the witness and said: "Fear Allah and be *just* in dealing with your children."[84]

SKEPTIC? SIMPLE ANSWERS USING QURAN AND SCIENCE

Indonesian Muslim kid is reading the Quran

Zulm Against Parents

Elderly parents are often sick, frail, and irritable. They lose their good looks and disposition, and caring for them involves time and effort. This makes aged parents vulnerable, particularly when they are dependent on their independent adult children. The Quran provides protection for elderly parents against both physical and emotional abuse, ensuring that their rights are safeguarded, **"You shall be kind to your parents; if one or both of them live to their old age in your lifetime, you shall not say to them any word of contempt nor repel them, and you shall address them [with] kind words"** (17:23).

Zulm Of Violating the Privacy of An Individual

Islam protects the privacy and other rights of an individual in several ways. Here are just three examples:
1. **Do not spy on one another** (49:12).
2. **Do not backbite about one another** (49:12).
3. **O believers! Do not enter houses other than your own until you have sought permission** (24:27).

No Suffering in Worship Rituals

Allah does not mandate any worship ritual which is extremely difficult or impossible to perform. Ritual fasting from dawn to dusk is so crucial that it is considered one of the five pillars of Islam. Breaking the fast before dusk is a sin. But suppose, while fasting, a person becomes too sick to continue and must break the fast to avoid a health crisis. Does this make the person a sinner? No. Fasting and other worship rituals are essential, but only if they do not cause undue hardship: **"Allah never wishes injustice to his creation"** (40:31).

> Islam adapts its own rules based on different circumstances to prevent oppression.

Those who are too old or sick to fast do not have to do so. They have the option to donate to charity or otherwise make up a missed fast. No person is responsible for anything beyond his/her capability.

Islam does not expect a Muslim priest to observe lifelong sexual abstinence. Instead, Muslim priests are supposed to get married. Similarly, Muslim are not required to leave society to seek personal enlightenment or to shun the world. Muslims should engage in daily activities as long as they avoid sin/zulm.

Zulm Of Self-Destructive Habits

Substance abuse, gambling, and playing the lottery are all self-destructive habits that harm individuals, families, and society. All such activities are prohibited in Islam: **"O believers! Intoxicants and gambling ... and division by arrows (lottery) are the filthy works of satan"** (5:90).

Taking Control of Negative Emotions

What about *self-inflicted psychological zulm*? What would happen if someone allowed negative emotions like anger, depression, guilt, and fear to persist instead of doing his/her best to be happy and peaceful? The problem may not be socially contagious, but an individual can privately suffer. For sure, Allah would be aware. Therefore, *avoidable zulm on one's own self is a sin, and consequently, it is prohibited.* A Muslim should seek Allah's help and continuously do his/her personal best to be happy, peaceful, and contented. Those Muslims who achieve this desirable goal are said to have *nafse mutmainna*, or **"fully satisfied soul"** (89:27). On the Day of Judgment, they will enter Paradise: **"Return to your Lord, [you are] well-pleased with Him, and He [Allah] is also pleased with you"** (89:28).

However, life's ups and downs present all kinds of challenges to our inner peace. The good news is that Islam teaches us how to achieve this incredible goal. For example, Prophet Muhammad[PBUH] taught a prayer for inner peace: "O Allah! I seek refuge with You from worry and grief, from incapacity and laziness, from cowardice and miserliness, from being heavily in debt and from being overpowered by (other) men."[85] Islam provides solutions to *emotional* problems. Only one instance is described here:

Taking Control of Negative Emotions: Controlling Anger

Allah says: **"When they [the righteous Muslims] are angry, they forgive"** (42:37). This verse not only points out the problem of anger, it provides the solution: *forgiveness*. If left unchecked, anger can torment our minds for decades, long after a provocative event has ended. This means we must try our best to forgive. At times, it may involve personal sacrifice and difficult adjustment. Forgiving and forgetting can often lead to healthier relationships.

The Prophet[PBUH] suggested that if you find it difficult to forgive some offender, then pray for that person and ask Allah to forgive the offender. This removes suppressed anger from the heart.

Amazing Solution: Islam Allows Realistic Exceptions

What if someone hurts you so deeply that you never want to associate with that offender or see him/her again? Perhaps the emotional wounds are too severe to heal. There can be another valid reason: what if the offender commits the same offense again?

These situations cause a conflict: (1) Islam insists on forgiveness, but (2) in some cases, if a victim makes up with the offender, the victim would be doing *zulm on self* (as in the two cases described in the previous paragraph). Zulm of self is also prohibited in Islam. In such situations, how does one forgive without doing zulm on self? Is this an impossible riddle to solve?
The beauty of Islam is that it offers a *practical solution* to this riddle. As the Quran suggests, in your *heart*, you forgive the offender. But if you are uncomfortable, you do not have to tell the offender. Also, if you are not emotionally ready, you do not have to associate or socially makeup with the offender because that would cause zulm on yourself.
We all have human limitations. At times, we are simply unable to associate with the offender. In the Battle of Uhud, the pagan Wahshi ibn Harb killed Hamza, who was a Muslim and the Prophet's uncle. Later, Wahshi ibn Harb converted to Islam. The Prophet[PBUH] welcomed him into Islam, *forgave him, and did not punish* him for the heinous murder. However, the Prophet[PBUH] said that he still did not wish to see Wahshi ibn Harb's face.

APPENDIX - A

In other words, forgive in your heart, but if you are uncomfortable, you have the right to keep the offender out of your life.

If you follow the Quran's advice, handling your anger becomes a win-win situation. In both situations, you save yourself from zulm. In summary:

(1) you forgive the offender in your heart. Islam regards your forgiveness as a good deed. Your anger fades away.
(2) You still have the freedom to decide if you want to socially make up with the offender.

What a beautiful yet practical solution?

Zulm on Animals

In Islamic justice, animals are also protected. Owners are responsible for treating their pets humanely. Prophet Muhammad[PBUH] said: "A woman entered Hell because of a cat which she had tied, neither giving it food nor setting it free to eat from the pests of the Earth."

Besides physical abuse, Prophet Muhammad[PBUH] also prohibited the mental abuse of animals. He instructed that if you plan to slaughter an animal to eat its meat, do not sharpen the knife where the animal can see it. Also, before the slaughter, ensure the knife is sharp to reduce the animal's suffering.[86]

No Self-Imposed Financial Suffering

Islam strongly advocates charity. A form of charity, *zakat*, is one of the five pillars of Islam. But what if a person donates all their worldly possessions and becomes bankrupt? That would be a financial disaster for the donor and his/her family. This will likely lead to self-pity and regret, a form of emotional suffering. For that reason, both self-imposed emotional and financial suffering are prohibited because Allah praises **"those who, when they spend, are not extravagant and not niggardly, but hold a just (balance) between those (extremes)"** (25:67). How carefully Islam guides the believers to avoid zulm in different areas of life?

Not Protecting Oneself from the Zulm of Others

When a Muslim has a choice, s/he is *required* to avoid becoming a *victim of zulm*. Allah praises those who **"defend themselves when wronged"** (26:227).

How do you defend yourself from the zulm of others? Islam provides strict guidelines. The first step is to exhaust all nonviolent options to protect yourself from zulm. One excellent example of this comes from the Treaty of Hudaybia. With profound insight, Prophet Muhammad[PBUH] saved Muslims from an all-out battle that would have caused heavy fatalities on both sides.

> With a remarkable nonviolent strategy, the Prophet[PBUH] convinced the Meccan pagans to sign the Treaty of Hudaybia and establish peace.

Depending on the circumstances, another option is to forgive the offender. And the last resort is for Muslims to use violence in self-defense. *However, Muslims are not allowed to exceed the original oppression caused by an offender.* That is because excessive aggression under the guise of defensive measures can lead to zulm on the offender.

What if a person is completely helpless to protect himself/herself from zulm? Islam regards such a person as a victim who is neither responsible for zulm-on-self nor a sinner. Victims of oppression should strive to protect themselves, remain hopeful and patient, and pray to Allah for relief. Allah promises forgiveness to helpless victims.

Miscellaneous types of zulm

Compassion is an indispensable part of Islam. Muslims must be sensitive to the feelings of fellow humans and respect their privacy. Here are a few examples of different types of zulm prohibited in Islam:

Muslims are instructed to give gifts to one another and accept gifts from others; they are not allowed to read other people's letters secretly and must be polite to everyone. After doing favors for others, Muslims are told not to advertise this or embarrass the recipients by reminding them of the favors. If someone asks for some favor or alms, a Muslim has only two options: help the needy or *politely* refuse. However, Muslims cannot humiliate a needy person or use sarcasm.

In summary, Islam prohibits zulm in all circumstances: **"Certainly the *Zalimun* [those who do zulm] will not be successful"** (6:135).

APPENDIX - A

How can our hearts find lasting peace?

With so much suffering in our lives and around us, can we still experience almost continuous peace and calm in our hearts? According to the Quran, the answer is yes, and the secret is: "**remembrance [Arabic word zikr used here] of God <u>certainly</u> brings comfort to <u>all hearts</u>**" (13:28). In Islam, the word *zikr* means 'remembering Allah.'

But the word *zikr* encompasses more than just remembering. According to the Muslim scholar Zainub Habib, "Dhikr is an all-embracing term that, in addition to including the ritual acts of worship, covers an array of activities of the tongue and heart. It involves thinking of and making mention of Allah at all times and in every area of our lives."[87] One example of zikr is performing the daily ritual supplications (salah), when a person communicates with Allah, both with body language and with words.

According to Habib, "This [zikr] is the worship that has no special time, but *is performed constantly* so that it permanently links up man's life with Allah and His service."[88] Ablution is not required to do zikr. "**Men who remember Allah standing, sitting and lying down on their sides and contemplate the (wonders of) creation …**" (3:191). This verse also tells us another method to remember Allah: by contemplating His miracles in the universe. By doing so, a believer feels closeness to Allah and promotes his/her own spiritual growth. Soon a stage comes when your heart is at peace. All the suffering in your life and around you feels distant and blurry:

> Something opens our wings.
> Something makes boredom and hurt disappear.
> Someone fills the cup in front of us.
> We taste only sacredness. ~ Rumi.

Sufi Rabia described zikr as:

> [Allah] Your hope in my heart is the rarest treasure
> Your Name on my tongue is the sweetest word
> My choicest hours
> Are the hours I spend with You -
> O God, I can't live in this world
> Without *remembering* You[89]

THEODICY: SUMMARY OF PARTS 1 AND 2

Even before humankind was created, Allah planned that humans would be sent to earth, where they would have many comforts and provisions. Allah also designed to test humans with various physical, financial, and emotional challenges. The whole scheme of Allah's test is carefully planned and customized for each individual. In worldly life, Allah only ordains what an individual can handle without getting overwhelmed or ruined. Allah also gives us the freedom to choose between good and evil.

Suffering and evil are part of Allah's test, but He also offers a complete road map for overcoming them. He has given us the guidance of the Islamic faith, worship rituals, prescribed charity and rules of ethics (like guidance to avoid zulm), and instructions on how to do zikr and to love unconditionally.

The tests of our worldly life have one clear goal: "**Allah wants to guide you, explain to you the customs of those who lived before you and grant you forgiveness**" (4:26). Even though we may be unaware, our hardships always have long-term benefits.

ACKNOWLEDGMENTS

I would like to express my gratitude to the talented artists and photographers whose work appears in this book:

Cover image: by Rudi Darmansyah (Astrology astronomy outer space big bang solar system planet galaxy creation. Elements of this image by NASA – Adobe Stock - nikonomad and Adobe Stock - Quran, the Islamic holy book by missisya)

Make it Easy – Shutterstock by phloxii
Epicurus – Shutterstock by Naci Yavuz
Homer – Shutterstock by Nickkey Nick
Xenophanes of Colophon – Shutterstock by Naci Yavuz
Mayan mythical god, Kinich Ahau – Shutterstock by NNNMMM
Isis, goddess of life and magic – Shutterstock by Gorbash Varvara
 Great Mosque in Sousse, Africa – Shutterstock by Ciesielski
Ibn Taymiyyah – Shutterstock by German Vizulis
In doubt – Shutterstock by ra2 studio
Good or bad intent – Shutterstock by Demidovich
Pandora – Shutterstock by Mikhail
Babylon ruins, Hillah, Iraq - Shutterstock by Cosmicos
Questions – Shutterstock by Carballo
Watch – Shutterstock by Naseer
Ibn Rushd - Shutterstock by Naci Yavuz
Charles Darwin – Shutterstock by Everett Collection
Evolution abstract illustration – Shutterstock by alionaprof
Damaged DNA - Shutterstock by Festa
Deep Space Elements of this image furnished by NASA – Shutterstock by Rolff
Rumi standing in a dark room – Shutterstock by slnyanar
Indonesian Muslim kid is reading the Quran – Shutterstock by Nami

Thank you for bringing beauty and inspiration to these pages.

NOTES

[1] Bitesize. (2023, 5 31). Retrieved from B.B.C.: https://www.bbc.co.uk/bitesize/guides/z43pfcw/revision/4

[2] This idea was proposed by Ibn Rushd. See Chapter 3.

[3] The Free Dictionary. [Online] [Cited: 8 16, 2017] ww.thefreedictionary.com/Pluralis+majestatis.

[4] Mishra, K. (2017, Sept 6). Then Why Call Him God? Retrieved from Indian Economy and Market: https://indianeconomyandmarket.com/2017/09/06/then-why-call-him-god/

[5] Fate or Free Will: "Odyssey" Book Discussion Questions. (2012, 1 26). Retrieved from DC Public Library: https://www.dclibrary.org/node/29604

[6] Qtd in Russell, Bertrand. History of Western Philosophy. Unwin Brothers, 1946. Print., p58-59

[7] Retrieved from Cambridge Dictionary: https://dictionary.cambridge.org/us/dictionary/english/anthropomorphism

[8] Tolle, Eckhart. A New Earth: Awakening to Your Life's Purpose. London. s.l. : Plume, a Penguin Group, 2005.

[9] J. B. Hare. The Internet Sacred Text Archive CD ROM 5.0 [CD-ROM] s.l. : The Internet Sacred Text Archive, 2005. ISBN-0-9709390-5-1.

[10] Encyclopedia Britannica. Hebrew patriarch. Encyclopedia Britannica [Online] 2016 [Cited: May 5, 2016.] read:http://www.britannica.com/biography/Jacob-Hebrew-patriarch.

[11] Telushkin, Joseph. Jewish Literacy page 22. New York: William Morrow and Company, 2008. ISBN 978-0061374982.

[12] The Concise Encyclopedia of Islam by Cyril Glasse, Page 141.

[13] Al-Mubarakpuri, Saifur Rahman. Ar Raheeq Al Makhtum. page 122.

[14] http://www.alim.org/library/quran/AlQuran-tafsir/MDD/1/0

[15] Hadees Qudsi #17

[16] Al-Ghazali, Imam. BELIEF IN GOD. The Jerusalem Treatise Excerpt from the The Revival of the Religious Sciences (Ihya' 'ulum al-din) [Online] [Cited: 5 10, 2016.]

[17] Translation by Malik

[18] Holtzman, Livnat. " Anthropomorphism." Encyclopedia of Islam, THREE. Edited by: Gudrun Krämer, Denis Matringe, John Nawas, Everett Rowson. Brill Online, 2013. Reference. 19 January 2013 <http://referenceworks.brillonline.com/entries/encyclopaedia

19 Different views on human freedom – Mu'tazilites and Asharites. (2022, 9 19). Retrieved from BBC: https://www.bbc.co.uk/bitesize/guides/zkdkw6f/revision/
20 Ibid.
21 Ibid.

[22] Albert Einstein Solves the Equation. LAPHAM'S Quarterly. [Online] [Cited: 7 23, 2017.] www.laphamsquarterly.org/religion/albert-einstein-solves-equation.

23 Frolov, Dmitry V.. " Freedom and Predestination." Encyclopaedia of the Qurʾān. Brill Online , 2013. Reference. Eeshat Ansari. 21 January 2013 <http://referenceworks.brillonline.com/entries/encyclopaedia-of-the-quran/freedom-and-predestination-SIM_00163>

[24] Ash'ari, A. (n.d.). In al Maqalat (p. 291). As quoted in www.muslimphilisophy.com/hmp/14.htm by Hye, M.A.

[25] Sunan Ibn Majah, Vol. 3, Book 10, Hadith 2044

[26] Sahih Al-Bukhari Hadith - 9.204

[27] Bukhari. Sahih Al-Bukhari 1.52 [CD ROM] Silver Spring, Maryland, USA : ISL Software Corporation, 1986-1999. Alim.

[28] Sahih Muslim 884.

[29] Al-Tirmidhi hadith # 1422.

[30] Sun. (2023, 2 8). Retrieved from National Geographic : https://education.nationalgeographic.org/resource/sun

[31] Bukhari [6.474]

[32] At-Tirmidhi. Question & Answers. Islamhelpline [Online] [Cited: May 15, 2016.] as recorded at http://www.islamhelpline.net/node/7905.

[33] Mishra, K. (2017, Sept 6). Then Why Call Him God? Retrieved from Indian Economy and Market: https://indianeconomyandmarket.com/2017/09/06/then-why-call-him-god/

[34] Sherry, P. (2021, 2 4). Theodicy. Retrieved from Encyclopedia of Britannica: www.britannica.com/topic/theodicy-theology

[35] Babylonian Philosophy – The Theodicy. (2021, 2 5). Retrieved from Thought Itself: https://ericgerlach.com/babylonian-philosophy-the-theodicy/

[36] (2021, 3 2). Retrieved from Successories: www.successories.com/iquote/author/13983/joseph-brodsky-quotes/2

[37] Ahmad, S. F. (2014). GOD, ISLAM & THE SKEPTIC MIND: A Study on Faith, Science, Religious Diversity, Ethics, and Evil. ISBN: 9781497360020

[38] Cosmological Argument. (2004, 7 13). Retrieved from Stanford Encyclopedia of Philosophy: https://plato.stanford.edu/entries/cosmological-argument/#HistOver

[39] Paley, W. (1800). Excerpts from William Paley's Natural Theology (1800). Retrieved from University of Oregon: https://pages.uoregon.edu/sshoemak/323/texts/william_paley.htm

[40] Coyne, R. D. (2005, Sep 1). One side can be wrong. Retrieved from The Guardian: https://www.theguardian.com/science/2005/sep/01/schools.research

[41] Hillier, H. C. (2023, 2 4). Ibn Rushd. Retrieved from IEP: https://iep.utm.edu/ibn-rushd-averroes

[42] Hawking, S. (2017). A Brief History of Time. New York: Bantam. doi:978-0553380163

[43] Ibid

[44] Khan, M. (2023, 12 2). Retrieved from The Quranic Arabic Corpus: https://corpus.quran.com/translation.jsp?chapter=5&verse=100

[45] Ayala, F. J. (2020, 11 20). Evolution. Retrieved from Britannica: https://www.britannica.com/science/evolution-scientific-theory

[46] Ibid.

[47] Evolution. (2020, 11 22). Retrieved from Science Daily: www.sciencedaily.com/terms/evolution.htm

[48] molecular biology: Additional Information. (23, 2 18). Retrieved from Encyclopedia of Britanica: https://www.britannica.com/science/molecular-biology

[49] Than, K. (2018, 2 27). What is Darwin's Theory of Evolution? Retrieved from LIVESCIENCE: https://www.livescience.com/474-controversy-evolution-works.html

[50] Retrieved from The Conversation: https://theconversation.com/natural-selection-in-black-and-white-how-industrial-pollution-changed-moths-43061

[51] MARON, D. F. (2018, 11 9). Under poaching pressure, elephants are evolving to lose their tusks. Retrieved from National Geographic: https://www.nationalgeographic.com/animals/article/wildlife-watch-news-tuskless-elephants-behavior-change

[52] Than, K. (2018, 2 27). What is Darwin's Theory of Evolution? Retrieved from LIVESCIENCE: https://www.livescience.com/474-controversy-evolution-works.html

[53] Ker Than, T. G. (2022, 10 14). What is Darwin's Theory of Evolution? Retrieved from Livescience: https://www.livescience.com/474-controversy-evolution-works.html

[54] Ibid.

[55] Ibid.

[56] Ibid.

[57] Pickrell, J. (2020, 11 22). Timeline: Human Evolution. Retrieved from New Scientist: https://www.newscientist.com/article/dn9989-timeline-human-evolution/

[58] Guessoum, Nidhal (2011). Islam's Quantum Question (p. 20). Bloomsbury Publishing. Kindle Edition.

[59] Ibid.

[60] Britannica, T. E. (2021, 10 18). Geocentric model. Retrieved from Encyclopaedia Britannica: https://www.britannica.com/science/geocentric-model

[61] Evolution. (n.d.). Retrieved from PBS: https://www.pbs.org/faithandreason/intro/evolu-frame.html
Pfahler, S. (2020, 12 13). Creationism and the Appearance of Age. Retrieved from University of South Dekota: http://apps.usd.edu/esci/creation/age/content/creationism_and_young_earth/appearance_of_age.html

[62] way to find exoplanets. Retrieved from The Conversation: theconversation.com/nobel-prize-in-physics-for-two-breakthroughs-evidence-for-the-big-bang-and-a-way-to-find-exoplanets-124930.

[63] Sciences, N. A. (1999). Science and Creationism. Retrieved from NCBI: https://www.ncbi.nlm.nih.gov/books/NBK230211/

[64] Jordan, S. (2020, 12 20). Origins of life: new evidence first cells could have formed at the bottom of the ocean. Retrieved from theconversation: https://theconversation.com/origins-of-life-new-evidence-first-cells-could-have-formed-at-the-bottom-of-the-ocean-126228

[65] Whitaker, B. (2009). In What's Really Wrong with the Middle East. Saqi Books From https://al-bab.com/islam-and-evolution (2020).

[66] DNA: Comparing Humans and Chimps. (2021, 3 8). Retrieved from American Museum of Natural History: www.amnh.org/exhibitions/permanent/human-origins/understanding-our-past/dna-comparing-humans-and-chimps

[67] Moran, G. (2020, 12 9). THE FINAL DOMINO: YASIR QADHI, YOUTUBE, AND EVOLUTION. Retrieved from Wiley Online Library: onlinelibrary.wiley.com/doi/full/10.1111/zygo.12666

[68] al-Mubarakpuri, Saifur Rahman. Ar-Raheeq Al-Makhtum.

[69] Qaribullah, P. H. (2022, 12 26). THE MILLENNIUM BIOGRAPHY OF MUHAMMAD. Retrieved from Mclean Ministries: https://www.mcleanministries.com/Biography.htm

[70] al-Mubarakpuri, Saifur Rahman. Ar-Raheeq Al-Makhtum.

[71] The world's fastest-growing religion is . CNN [Online] [Cited: May 28, 2016.] www.cnn.com/2015/04/02/living/pew-study-religion/.

[72] Long history with Islam gives Indigenous Australians pride. The Conversation US, Inc [Online] [Cited: May 28, 2016.] read:http://theconversation.com/long-history-with-islam-gives-indigenous-australians-pride-3521.

[73] Islam on march south of border. wnd tv [Online] [Cited: May 28, 2016.] http://www.wnd.com/2005/06/30674/.

[74] The Invocation of God. Ibn Qayyum al-Jawziyya. Translator: M. Abdurrahman Fitzgerald. The invocation of God by page 49. Cambridge. Islamic Texts Society. 2000. 0946621780.

[75] Fadiman and Frager. Essential of Sufism. page 119. New York. HarperCollins. 1997. 0785809066.

[76] Sahih Muslim 131.

[77] 37 Things Jalaluddin Rumi Can Teach You About Love. Purpose Fairy. [Online] [Cited: Oct. 7, 2019.] https://www.purposefairy.com/85691/things-jalaluddin-rumi-teach-love/.

[78] Encyclopaedia of Islam, Second Edition. Zulm. Brill Online [Online] [Cited: January 19, 2013.] http://referenceworks.brillonline.com/entries/encyclopaedia-of-islam-2/zulm-COM_1393.

[79] Ibid.

[80] Ibid.

[81] Lane, E.W. Arabic-English Lexicon. London. Willams & Norgate,1863. 9780946621033

[82] Dictionary of the Holy Quran by Abdul Mannan Omar page 351

[83] " Ẓulm." Encyclopaedia of Islam, Second Edition. Brill Online , 2013. Reference. Eeshat Ansari. 19 January 2013 <http://referenceworks.brillonline.com/entries/encyclopaedia-of-islam-2/zulm-COM_1393>

[84] al-Sheha Abdul-Rahma, Misconception on human rights on Islam, page 67. Riyadh.

[85] Bukhari 8.380

[86] Muslim, Hadith no. 910.

[87] Habib, Z. (2021, 4 15). Dhikr - Remembrance of Allah. Retrieved from Farhat Hashmi: https://www.farhathashmi.com/articles-section/remembrance/dhikr-remembrance-of-allah

[88] Ibid

[89] Rabia Basri. (n.d.). Retrieved from AZQuotes: https://www.azquotes.com/quote/593732

www.ingramcontent.com/pod-product-compliance
Lightning Source LLC
Chambersburg PA
CBHW070518100426
42743CB00010B/1852